Praise for *Underst*

This is a rich resource for leaders at al
authors use a range of national and i
resources which are accessible and ready for practical application.
questions at the start of each chapter and the self-review at the end of each chapter will help to support individual reflection, as well as provide stimuli for teams and coaching conversations. The authors challenge traditional assumptions about leadership, management, social equity and collaboration. They provide evidence for readers to construct alternative perspectives with the emphasis on the core business of learning and leadership for the future.

At the centre is the message that each learner, child or adult is unique. Around this fixed point the authors open up the layers of leadership and learning in each of the eight chapters. The book is valuable on many different levels; in supporting an individual leader to articulate their personal construct of leadership, through to supporting a leadership programme as a core text. The book provides a coherent and logical framework for examining leadership – individuals and teams can use it to tell their leadership story.

Carolyn Hughan, Director, ETC Teaching School Alliance

Understanding Leadership could not have been written at a better time! School leaders across all sectors and in all areas of school life are going through a time of substantial change and uncertainty. Indeed many leaders at the moment are wondering how and if they will be able to adapt at all.

Understanding Leadership is the perfect antidote to all this uncertainty and an excellent resource for leaders at all levels and across all sectors. In fact, one of the main points that the book makes is that 'virtually all the ideas and principles discussed in this book apply to everyone who works in the school community', as the authors are very clear that leadership 'should be regarded as a collective capacity rather than the status of the few'.

The book sets out very clearly the reasons why leaders in education play such a vital role in society. In each chapter the authors do an excellent job of enthusing and inspiring practitioners at all levels with the potential for good that exists within the various remits of leadership.

It would be difficult to find another book that sets out the principles, philosophies, challenges and theories of leadership with such clarity, with so many excellent sources to illustrate various trains of thought and with so many opportunities for self-reflection and for re-energising one's own practice.

The way that Libby Nicholas and John West-Burnham have written this book gives the reader a very clear picture of the principles that underpin each of the ideas and ways of being. They also provide the reader with a very clear understanding of how these ideas may look in practice and the benefits that one would see having established them within one's own organisation. The book makes aiming for certain goals, certain cultures and certain ways of being a really plausible proposition: time and time again I found myself reflecting on how much sense the concepts make. It is fascinating how the authors are so skilled in placing leadership within the context of society and of real-life scenarios by emphasising the link between leadership and moral purpose throughout the book.

The book is structured in such a way that it would make the perfect accompaniment to school improvement – three year school strategic plans could easily be based on the principles outlined. INSET days, away days, CPD could all be very easily aligned around the structure of each of the chapters. I cannot wait to look at my own short, medium and long term strategic plans, together with our whole school professional development and philosophy of education now, and begin to adapt these to match the sequence of the chapters in this book. Indeed the authors place great emphasis on the symbiotic relationship between leadership and learning and, very interestingly, note that 'leadership in education exists to enable learning'.

The book is also excellent at linking the various theories and ideas with not only current pressures but also with exciting opportunities that the current climate is bringing to educationalists. The sections on learning, partnerships and evidence-based practice could not be better set out and the words of wisdom within these chapters stand out as an absolute must for all leaders of today.

The book is very informative and it is written in a way that enables the reader to reflect, think, question, hypothesise, wonder and, at the same time, be inspired and feel skilled and equipped to design and put next steps into practice. The way the book focuses on the personal qualities of successful leaders is hugely impressive and, I feel, will be quite transformational. The authors make an excellent and quite unique link between love and leadership, to remind the reader that 'the current emphasis on performativity and competition has to be reconciled with the centrality of effective human relationships'.

It is a book that school leaders will have both as a quick reference point whenever they need inspiration and ideas and as an essential tool that enables them to think strategically to drive their own visions and create learning climates where all children are able to maximise their potential.

Marcelo Staricoff, Head Teacher, Balfour Primary School

Understanding Leadership provides the reader with a range of illuminating opportunities to seriously think and reflect on his or her effectiveness as a leader in responding to the fundamental challenges in schools today. The text is characterised by regular opportunities for personal review and a series of challenging, and sometimes provocative, questions. This is a must-read for any school leader operating within the current constantly changing educational landscape.

Leanne Eyre, Director of Professional Learning,
University of Chester Academies Trust

Understanding Leadership is an excellent resource for anyone who is interested in the importance of school leadership. The book invites us to refocus on the reasons why we chose to be involved in school leadership through its relentless focus on learning. The regular opportunities to reflect on our own and others' practice through frequent questioning certainly challenges us to adapt and refine our approach to school leadership. The authors skilfully encourage us all to develop our professional practice, which is an essential requirement as we seek to navigate our way through an uncertain educational landscape.

Mark Vickers, CEO, Olive Academies Trust

UNDERSTANDING LEADERSHIP

Challenges and reflections

Libby Nicholas
John West-Burnham

Crown House Publishing Limited
www.crownhouse.co.uk

Originally published in hardback (ISBN 978-178583026-6)

First published in paperback by

Crown House Publishing Limited
Crown Buildings, Bancyfelin, Carmarthen, Wales, SA33 5ND, UK
www.crownhouse.co.uk

and

Crown House Publishing Company LLC
PO Box 2223, Williston, VT 05495, USA
www.crownhousepublishing.com

British Library Cataloguing-in-Publication Data

A catalogue entry for this book is available from the British Library.

Print ISBN 978-178583026-6 (Hardback)
Print ISBN 978-178583334-2 (Paperback)
Mobi ISBN 978-178583066-2
ePub ISBN 978-178583067-9
ePDF ISBN 978-178583068-6

LCCN 2015953346

Printed and bound in the UK by
TJ International, Padstow, Cornwall

For

Isabella Nicholas

Elizabeth and Imogen West-Burnham

Contents

Introduction

The purpose of this book is to act as a resource to support your personal review and reflection on your effectiveness as a leader. Throughout the book we have tried to provide you with a range of ideas, research and information that will provide a stimulus for your thinking. Our approach is deliberately challenging and we make no apology for what might be seen as somewhat confrontational language and questioning.

Challenge is one of the most significant factors in effective learning. In many respects we follow Socrates in his use of the aphorism 'know thyself' and the assertion at his trial that 'the unexamined life is not worth living'. Leadership cannot be taught; it has to be learnt. Questioning, interrogating and analysing ideas and practice are fundamental to that learning process. This book is not an academic text, nor is it a self-help manual. We hope that it is both intellectually coherent and challenging, and professionally relevant and supportive.

We have tried to draw on an eclectic range of sources to encourage as many alternative perspectives as possible. Generally, we have tried to use evidence-based sources, although sometimes we have drawn on anecdotal insights and personal observations as well as the occasional indulgent polemic.

The distinctive nature of this book is the regular opportunities it provides to stop reading and review and reflect on the messages and implications for your understanding of leadership. At frequent intervals the text is interspersed with questions, challenges and opportunities for personal reflection, and each chapter ends with a structured review to help identify your strengths and possible areas for development. Equally, we hope that you will find this book to be a useful resource in your work with your coach and as part of your appraisal process. Some of the topics might well lend themselves to supporting collaborative learning opportunities through shared review and reflection.

It might also be worth considering keeping a journal as an aid to review and reflection as you read through the book. We recognise that for some this is the most natural process and for others it can be contrived and artificial. We hope that our approach is helpful and facilitates your thinking about the process of reflection as much as about the themes of that reflection.

We are not academically or professionally neutral; we strongly believe that the dominant themes informing educational leadership are to do with the key issue of equity in all its various permutations. This directly influences our choice of themes and resources, although we believe that almost all of the book is relevant to a range of contexts and systems.

The following questions, themes and topics underpin the eight chapters in this book:

1. Why leadership?

- Understanding the origins of prevailing models of leadership.
- Recognising the problems with certain approaches to leadership in education.
- Justifying the models of leadership prevalent in schools.
- Developing a common language to enable shared understanding of effective leadership.

2. Creating a preferred future – leading change

What is the evidence that your leadership has a strategic perspective?

- Creating a culture of aspiration and hope.
- Moving from improving to transforming.
- Developing strategic conversations.

- Building preferred scenarios.
- Leading change and innovation.

3. Leadership as a moral activity

How does your leadership create a culture and practice based on shared values?

- Building a moral consensus focused on securing equity.
- Working through authenticity and integrity.
- Considering how successful leaders make decisions.
- Focusing on 'doing the right things' as a leader.
- Holding colleagues to account.

4. Learning as the core purpose of school leadership

What do leaders do to secure effective learning for all?

- Embedding the principles of effective learning.
- Realising potential through personalisation.
- Focusing on teaching to close the gap.
- Enabling progress in learning and so achievement for all.
- Emphasising evidence and data-based teaching and learning.

5. Leading through collaboration and cooperation

How far is leadership based on cooperation and collaboration?

- Moving from autonomy to collaborative working – bonding to bridging.
- Developing social capital.
- Looking at leadership beyond the school – across the system.
- Focusing on intervention to prevent failure.

6. Building capacity – sharing leadership

Is leadership about personal status or collective capacity?

- Moving from dependency to interdependency.
- Building a culture of trust and empowerment.
- Progressing from distributed to shared leadership.
- Securing leadership capacity and sustainability.

7. Leading through relationships

In what ways does leadership work through sophisticated personal relationships?

- Focusing on the rational–emotional continuum of leadership.
- Understanding leadership through love and power.
- Leading through trust and empathy.
- Encouraging a commitment to care and compassion.
- Developing emotional literacy.

8. Leadership and personal resilience

How is effective leadership nurtured and sustained?

- Fostering strategies for personal growth and development.
- Developing personal well-being – 'reservoirs of hope'.
- Advocating resilience and sustainability.

Chapter 1

Why leadership?

There seems to be a broad consensus across educational systems that leadership is a key variable in educational improvement. There is less consensus as to the exact nature of successful leadership and the direction that leadership in education might take. This chapter explores the following issues:

- Why is there such an emphasis on leadership?
- What are the origins of the prevailing models of leadership in education?
- What are the problems and issues with certain approaches to leadership in education?
- Can we justify the prevailing models of leadership found in schools?
- Is there a common language to enable a shared understanding of effective leadership?

The problem with leadership

There seems little doubt that leadership is a highly significant factor in explaining the success or otherwise of a school or indeed any human social enterprise. Leadership has always been a vital element in any school improvement strategy, and all the research evidence points to certain types of leadership behaviour as being essential to turning schools around. Indeed, it would seem that there is an overwhelming consensus not just about the importance of leadership but also about the specific components of that leadership:

> A large number of quantitative studies ... show that school leadership influences performance more than any other variable except socio-economic background and the quality of teaching. (Barber et al. 2010: 5)

This assertion has, of course, to be qualified from a number of perspectives: the historical context and prevailing culture of the school, the leadership styles and strategies adopted and, crucially in a high stakes accountability model, the relative impact of the leader.

What is very clear is that there is an increasing focus on what might be described as a 'managerial perspective' in government, across the public sector and in education. This is reflected in neoliberal stances on the importance of competition, the absence of central control, the emphasis on autonomy and the increasing stress on technical expertise as being more significant than any concept of community accountability or institutional or local democracy.

However, Pink (2008: 2) argues:

> We are moving from an economy and a society built on the logical, linear, computerlike capabilities of the Information Age to an economy and a society built on the inventive, empathic, big-picture capabilities of what's rising in its place, the Conceptual Age.

If this is true, then it would seem to imply the need for a radical reconceptualisation of the prevailing models of leadership. But the history of the West has tended to stress the individuality of leadership and regard leadership as, in some way, intrinsically heroic. This has been reinforced, not least in schools, by a parallel culture of dependency (waiting to be saved by the hero) rather than the more complex and demanding concept of followership (accepting responsibility for co-creating a preferred future). It might be that one type of relationship between learner and teacher, essentially dependent, is a microcosm of the relationship between head teacher and staff. In order to respond to the challenges of living in a very different world, leadership may need to be understood as a process and a relationship rather than personal status and a reified position posited on degrees of significance and value:

> our understanding of leadership needs to move beyond contemplation of isolated heroes and consider instead those who translate their ideas into action ... in order to understand how individual leaders and followers contribute to the leadership process we need to understand and explain how their psychologies are shaped and transformed by their engagement in shared group activity. (Haslam et al. 2011: 17)

The crucial point here is that leadership is derived from significant relationships – that is, leadership is a function of the social and emotional dynamics of the group. It is not so much a matter of the leader taking control of the group but rather understanding the emotional climate of which they have become a part. The reality is, of course, that leadership is a fundamentally contested concept. It is a fuzzy and highly complex set of interconnected propositions that are not amenable to a technical-rational interpretation. The leader as technician is as potentially dangerous as the leader as hero. Clearly, there needs to be a balance between leadership as a set of technical skills and leadership as an art rooted in relationships, imagination and moral purpose.

Is the Anglophone world in thrall to the idea of the hero-leader?

Is this a cultural issue or a manifestation of a dependency culture?

Do we still believe that charisma is a helpful concept in talking about leadership in education?

What are the implications of the move towards academisation and increased collaboration for our understanding of effective leadership?

Can leadership be reduced to a set of technical skills?

In their study of the potential implications of the development of various types of technology on the nature, status and work of professionals, Susskind and Susskind (2015: 32) identify a number of key questions:

1. Might there be entirely new ways of organising professional work that are more affordable, more accessible and perhaps more conducive to an increase in quality than traditional approaches?

2. Does it follow that *all* the work that our professionals currently do can only be undertaken by licensed experts?

3. To what extent do we actually trust professionals to admit that their services could be delivered differently?

4. Are our professions fit for purpose? Are they serving our societies well?

If the word 'professional' is replaced with 'leaders' then a powerful and potentially challenging critique begins to emerge. This critique is powerfully expressed in the conclusion of their analysis in which they see two possible ways forward:

> One leads to a society in which practical expertise is a shared online resource, freely available and maintained in a collaborative spirit. The other route leads to a society in which this knowledge and experience may be available online, but is owned and controlled by providers. (Susskind and Susskind 2015: 307)

This is the essential dilemma about the nature of leadership: is it to be seen as a collective capacity working through shared ownership and interdependency, or is it about control and the exercise of power? Brown (2014: 9) extends this critique of a world dominated by an essentially historical view of leadership:

> 'Strong' leadership is, then, generally taken to signify an individual concentrating power in his or her own hands and wielding it decisively. Yet the more power and authority is accumulated in just one leader's hands, the more that leader comes to believe in his or her unrivalled judgement and indispensability.

An important corollary of this, Brown argues, is that leaders are overwhelmed by the number of decisions they are required to take and so either delegate inappropriately or make rushed decisions on the basis of inadequate evidence. Strong leaders are often guilty of the rationalistic fallacy – the belief that the world is controllable, predictable and essentially linear. Of course, nothing could be further from the truth. Leadership is messy and swampy and the idea that effective leaders can occupy the high ground and actually control their world is part of the mythology of strong leadership.

Brown goes on to make the case for moving away from the emphasis on the leader to recognising that they 'must be able to appeal to emotion, sharing in the sense of identity of their party or group' (Brown 2014: 61). This is about much more than building effective teams, working through consensus or developing quality relationships. Rather, it is about moving away from focusing on the leader and questioning the very concept of the leader-centric organisation. For Haslam et al. (2011: 17) leadership is too often seen:

> as a noun rather than as a verb, something that leaders possess rather than as a process in which they are participants ... leader-centricity tends to obscure, if not completely overlook, the role that followers play.

An interesting example of the cultural implications of a leader-centricity is the way in which orchestral conductors are perceived. The most famous (but not all) seem to be characterised by a combination of supreme musicianship and massive egos. There is no doubt that individual conductors can make an enormous difference to a performance – the difference between a competent performance and a life-changing event. And yet orchestral musicians are extraordinarily technically accomplished; most, if not all, are capable of solo performances of the highest standard. So, is the conductor just another manifestation of the need to have a leader rather than explore different ways of working? Consider the following characteristics of the work of professional orchestral musicians:

- Recruitment to a great orchestra requires the highest possible combination of technical mastery and musicianship.
- Each section of the orchestra and the whole ensemble spend hours in rehearsal in addition to personal practice.
- Orchestras develop a unique 'voice' in terms of their approach to the orchestral repertoire and could perform many pieces irrespective of what the conductor might be doing.

It would be wrong to be overly naive or idealistic about the ability of highly accomplished musicians to be self-directing. It is doubtful if a Mahler symphony could be performed without strong central direction; likewise, the micro-politics of some trios and quartets can be feral at best.

This emphasis on the leader as an individual is expressed in a wide variety of ways, not least the widening gap between leaders and followers in terms of status, remuneration and rewards. The range of remuneration – the difference between the highest and lowest paid people in an organisation – provides an interesting insight into the values of that organisation. It is often claimed that this gap is necessary and justified because of the increasing accountability that is focused on the individual and the competition to secure the most effective leaders. But this, of course, is a reinforcing factor that merely compounds the issue.

> How can it be possible in any human enterprise, let alone a school, to identify and isolate the contribution of one individual to the exclusion of all others?
>
> To what extent is your school leader centric?
>
> Does your school's leadership subscribe to the rationalistic fallacy?
>
> How is your perspective on the nature of successful leadership reflected in the way that your school functions?
>
> How might information technology influence the future of the leadership of the teaching profession?

There is a possibility that the hero-leader in a leader-centric society might actually inhibit or distort democratic processes, innovation and cooperation. These concerns are exacerbated by issues surrounding the possibility of actually training or developing the relational dimensions of leadership:

> We think that leadership can be taught – which, given the paucity of objective evidence, might be true or might not. We think that leadership can be learned quickly and easily ... We think leader-centrically – that being a leader is better and more important than being a follower. Wrong again. (Kellerman 2012: xx)

The discussion in this chapter is intended to apply to anyone who has a responsibility to provide leadership – in the classroom, for the team, for the school, trust or federation. There is a real danger in education that leadership is seen as essentially synonymous with headship and that other manifestations of leading in the school are essentially derivative or diluted versions of leadership.

A major issue at the outset of this discussion is that there are multiple alternative definitions and permutations of leadership (at least 25 in MacBeath's 2004 study) and it is possible to get totally bewildered in the semantics of the concept. It is essentially a Humpty Dumpty word – it means whatever we want it to mean.

Leadership is defined by context, culture and, occasionally, by evidence. However, it is also determined by personality and political forces, and some of the most effective leaders – by a range of criteria – have been some of the most evil people in history. Equally challenging is the very mixed academic provenance of leadership – it draws on a wide range of academic disciplines in what is often seen as an essentially parasitic way, with no real attempt at an intellectually coherent synthesis or an integrated conceptual framework. So elements from psychology, sociology, economics and politics all go into the pot. The mixture is then complicated by the introduction of historic perspectives combined with insights from social anthropology and theology:

> So, despite the contribution of scientific enquiry we have recourse to our own assumptions, philosophies, values and religious beliefs. These are what drive our behaviour, shape our relationships and ultimately determine what, where and how children and young people learn. (MacBeath 2004: 3)

It is therefore essential that leaders are continually testing and clarifying their assumptions and philosophies. There can be no definitive overarching model of effective leadership that achieves universal consensus; discussions about the nature of leadership will always be exploratory, never definitive. There are numerous variables that will inform and influence how any leader perceives their role – gender, ethnicity and personal influences, such as family life and educational experiences, are all very real and powerful factors.

Running parallel with recognising and analysing all of the complex variables that inform personal decisions about how to lead are the processes by which leaders make sense of and apply their chosen approach. This alerts us to the fact that leadership is essentially a personal construct – a mental map or a mindscape – that helps us to make sense of the world and determines our choices and behaviour. One of the most significant ways in which we can each change and develop our mental maps is through reflection and review – hence the approach that we have adopted in this book.

> What would you see as the most significant factors influencing your personal model of effective leadership?
>
> Are you naturally directive/assertive, analytical/autonomous, altruistic/nurturing or a combination of all? Is there a balance of these leadership characteristics in your senior team?
>
> You might consider drawing a pie chart showing the relative contribution of the variables that you see as being the most significant in determining your own personal mental map of leadership.

There is no shortcut to developing personal confidence as a leader. The issue of how theory is translated into practice is one of the most challenging aspects of any form of professional practice. Given the complexity of the provenance of leadership, it might be seen as too problematic a concept and therefore it is easier to follow a deficit model of effective management operating under the guise of leadership. However, it may be possible to apply Occam's razor and offer a model of leadership that is simple but nevertheless includes all the important elements.

What seems to be the case is that the prevailing models of leadership, irrespective of culture or context, have four key factors in common: the principles or values informing the nature of leadership, the core purpose or focus that clarifies the nature of the business, the human relationships that define how the organisation works, and the policies and practice that convert principle into concrete practice. They might be defined in detail as follows:

- Principle: Leadership is an essentially moral activity; leaders have a responsibility to support the development of real consensus around the core values that inform the way in which the school works. Leaders make decisions and these choices have to be consistent with the moral framework that has been agreed. There does seem to be evidence that the clarity and consistency of the moral framework has a direct impact on organisational performance.
- Purpose: Leaders are responsible for defining and clarifying the core business of the organisation and its future direction by articulating possible future scenarios and securing engagement and commitment – often summed up in the memorable phrase, 'keeping the herd heading roughly west'. For schools, this is a crucial function: is the

core purpose of the school to optimise academic attainment, or to secure the development of personal well-being? The two are not incompatible, but it does seem to be a challenge to reconcile academic attainment with a humanistic model of education and grant them equal status.

- People: Leadership can only work through effective human relationships. Leaders model emotional literacy and work on the motivation and engagement of all staff. Effective leaders recognise the emotional dimension of work and endeavour to create a culture that is based on respect for the dignity of every member of the school community. Leaders build a shared language to facilitate communication and design organisational structures that support effective relationships (e.g. self-managing teams).
- Policies: Leaders develop policies and strategies that translate principle into practice. Through the development of management structures and processes, they ensure that aspirations and plans are supported by operational routines which are consistently and efficiently applied. At the heart of the policies component lies issues around monitoring, efficiency, value for money and ensuring that the school is safe and working to optimum effect.

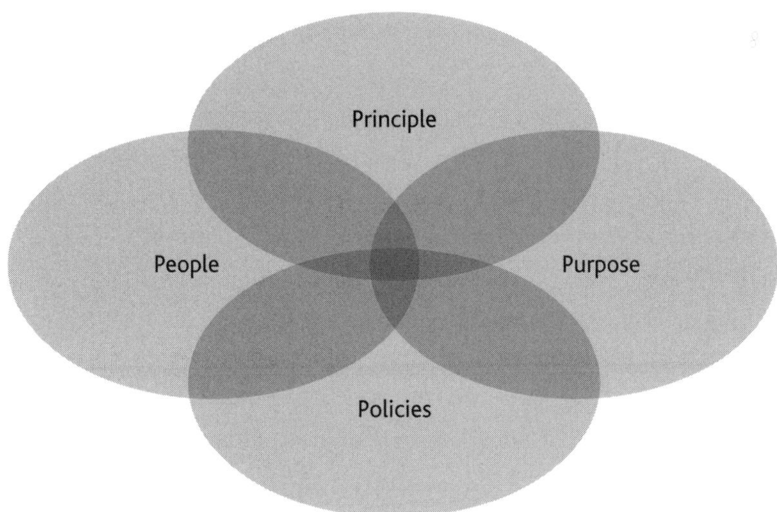

Figure 1.1. The components of effective leadership

Successful leaders are those people who can integrate the 4 P's, so they are balanced and mutually supportive – as shown in Figure 1.1. Highly effective leadership is most likely to occur when the circles overlap and the four elements become interdependent.

We need to consider the implications of individuals in leadership roles who do not possess each of these elements in an appropriate balance. In reality, we will always be aiming for the optimum level of integration. However, it would be naive to pretend that it is in any way easy or normal to find people with these characteristics. This is why consciously developing leadership capacity is so important – effective leadership can be learnt, and this is why it is necessary to build confidence and extend personal capacity by developing an understanding of how leadership works.

Consider the leader who has clear principles and purpose but is unable to engage with people. What about the leader who is clear about purpose and good with people but has no real sense of principle? Or what about the leader who is engaged with people and principle but has no sense of purpose, or who lacks clear focus or direction? Finally, what about the leader who is unable to translate principle and purpose into meaningful systems and processes? Clearly, the permutations could be explored ad infinitum, but it is apparent that any leader who does not engage with all four elements is likely to be highly dysfunctional.

> Is it worth testing the 4 P's model against those leaders who you admire most, be they religious, historical, political or community leaders?
>
> What is it about them that makes them special from your perspective?
>
> Using the 4 P's model, reflect on school leaders you have known. Does the model help to explain aspects of their relative effectiveness or lack of effectiveness?
>
> What happens when somebody in a leadership role lacks one of the four elements?

Once a working definition of leadership is achieved (i.e. the four components of the 4P's model) then it becomes possible to develop confidence in recognising those aspects of the work of a school leader that do *not* constitute leadership. The classic distinction, and a potential semantic battleground, is the relationship between leadership and management. Both are necessary and their relationship should be one of mutual support with a high degree of interdependence, but always within the context of clear leadership. The danger arises when management, and even worse managerialism, becomes the dominant culture. One way of understanding the relationship between leadership and management is to define their relative contributions to the way in which an organisation functions. It is also worth introducing routine administrative work into the equation as it plays an important role in the life of every school.

Leadership	Management	Administration
Doing the right things	Doing things right	Doing things
Path making	Path following	Path tidying
Engaging with complexity	Creating clarity	Securing consistency

Table 1.1. Leadership, management and administration

In Table 1.1, we can see that, firstly, leadership is about having responsibility for the values by which the school works – 'doing the right things' in Bennis' famous phrase (Bennis and Nanus 1985: 21). What the right things are is highly contestable and will be the product of personal values, the prevailing moral consensus in society and the shared values of the school. In many ways, leadership might be best understood as a process of decision making – with some choices obvious and easy and others complex and challenging. Management, by contrast, is concerned with translating principles into actual practice or 'doing things right' – focusing on systems, structures and delivery. In essence, ensuring that the ideal and the aspirational is made concrete. Administration is about doing all the basic tasks – the organisational routines and infrastructure. All three are necessary in order to ensure that the school is living by its principles.

Secondly, leadership is concerned with setting the purpose and direction of the school, defining the path forward in the very powerful image defined by Covey (1992: 101) – articulating what the school actually exists to do and how it should be in the future. Path following ensures that the journey is actually possible. After the dreamers come the builders. Management is about ensuring that the purpose is reflected across the organisation in its day-to-day working and that everything works. The aspiration for an inclusive school requires a great deal of hard work to deliver a safe and effective learning environment for all. Administrative work ensures that everything is in place – that the path is kept tidy.

Thirdly, leadership is fundamentally concerned with the complexity of human relationships, performance, engagement and motivation – leadership has to be seen as relational. Leadership only exists in the extent to which there is emotional engagement and sophisticated interpersonal relationships. Management is about the deployment of staff, the allocation of resources and delivery, with administration providing the consistency to support all these other factors.

Leadership	**Management**
Transformation	Improvement
Trust	Control
Questioning	Accepting
Creativity	Conformity
Relationships/emotions	Systems/structures
Values	Standards
Innovation	Continuity
Coaching	Training

Table 1.2. The vocabulary of leadership and management

Table 1.2 provides another way of exploring the relationship between leadership and management. The words chosen imply significant value judgements, but one of the key elements in individual leadership development – and successful leadership in any organisation – is the creation of a working vocabulary that supports meaningful dialogue and the development of shared meaning. Precisely what any of these terms mean will be determined by local custom and practice and by the formation, over time, of a common value system leading to a detailed and sophisticated common language.

It is perhaps worth noting in passing that the management column in Table 1.2 contains many words that are associated with so-called 'left hemisphere' thinking and the leadership column has many words linked with 'right hemisphere' thinking. Although the brain does not actually work as two distinct hemispheres (an important point about effective leadership in any context) but rather in an integrated way, there are clearly thought patterns in which the logical/rational dominates and thought patterns in which the emotional/creative dominates. Another perspective is that the management list is stereotypically masculine and the leadership qualities are essentially feminine. A list of this nature inevitably creates an artificial polarity – the truth, as always, lies between the extremes. However, the balance between management and leadership is fundamental to organisational success.

Which is worse:

- A school that is inspirationally led but badly managed?
- A school that is efficiently managed but badly led?
- A school where bureaucratic systems are more important than personal relationships?
- How does this perspective link with the model in Table 1.1?

Getting either leadership or management out of balance is clearly dysfunctional. The lack of one compromises the other, and the potential of each is inhibited by the failure to achieve interdependent working. The balance between leadership and management has to be determined by context and by the needs of the school at any given time. One of the great skills of highly effective leaders is to get the balance right – to find the optimum relationship that the school needs at a particular time.

There is little point in having inspirational, creative and transformative leadership if there is no infrastructure to convert it into practice. A great artist has to be able to create or a composer orchestrate. Equally, if management dominates then there will be bureaucratic neatness, efficiency and order but the school will be static – the means will be more important than the end. In the worst cases, a school will be dominated by a culture of managerialism where reductionist and instrumental strategies prevail.

There are a range of factors that determine the balance of management and leadership:

- The context of the school: Is it 'safe'? Is learning secure for all? Does it work in organisational and operational terms?
- Expectations of staff: Often it is easier, and more comfortable, to be managed rather than led. Leaders may be tempted to secure popularity by supporting through managing rather than challenging through leadership.
- External pressures: Implementation of national and local policies and strategies might lead to a culture of passive responsiveness (i.e. the management of policy rather than the development of creative and innovative responses to policy).
- Self-perception: Many people will be psychologically more comfortable with the role of manager rather than leader; the operational is more benign than the strategic.

Another perspective on the relationship between leading and managing is to return to the idea of mental maps – that is, how our constructs of the world act as a way of making sense and allowing us to negotiate, engage with, understand and seek to change the landscape that we inhabit. Sergiovanni (2005: 24) talks of mindscapes rather than mental maps. For him mindscapes are:

> implicit mental frames through which reality ... and our place in this reality are envisioned. Mindscapes provide us with intellectual and psychological images of the real world and boundaries and parameters of rationality that help us to make sense of this world ... mindscapes are intellectual security blankets ... and road maps through an uncertain world.

Each leadership mindscape is unique – the product of everything that makes us who we are. Effective leaders understand their mindscapes, work to systematically enrich and deepen them and use them to navigate their world. Becoming an effective leader might be seen as building rich personal mindscapes that enable alternative models of the future to emerge. Many of the key transitional phases in our personal and professional lives involve adjusting our mindscapes: from pupil to student to teacher, from being single to being in a relationship to being a parent, from being a follower to being a leader.

Cummings and Keen (2008: 12) extend the idea of the mindscape into a landscape analogy by exploring the issue of the relationship between private mindscapes and public landscapes. An adaptation of their model to school leadership, as a way of interpreting and understanding the context in which leaders have to work, is shown in Figure 1.2.

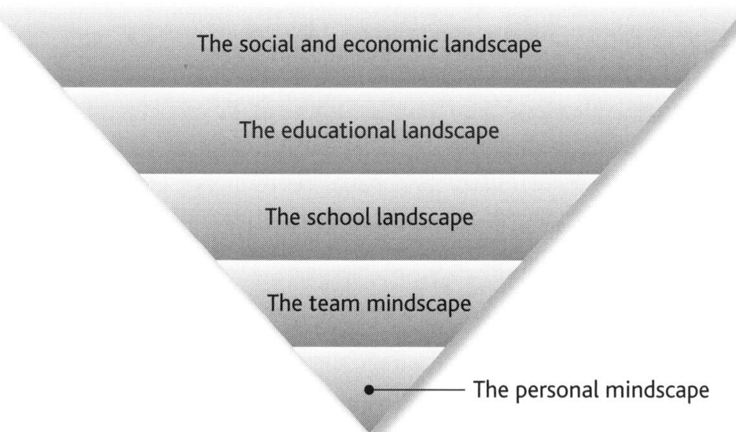

Figure 1.2. Mindscape into landscape

There are numerous ways of interpreting this particular model in order to explore and explain the relationship between the leader as an individual and the context in which she or he functions. In many ways, the important point about this approach is that the effective leader understands the relationship between their personal mindscape and the various landscapes they inhabit. This is the central issue in ensuring that leadership is appropriate to context and that leaders have the confidence to be able to respond to changing circumstances in a way that secures personal integrity with relevant and appropriate strategies.

> How has your mindscape changed over the years?
>
> To what extent is your personal mindscape of leadership appropriate to the context in which you work?
>
> What are the issues in translating your personal mindscape into a working landscape? Is there a tension between the context of education and your personal mindscape?
>
> How far does your team share your mindscape – are there tensions in terms of the fundamental assumptions underpinning how the team thinks and works?

Becoming a leader

If the nature of leadership is complex, problematic and elusive, then the nature of learning is even more so. Much of the popular discourse about learning characterises it as an essentially passive process, whether that is being taught, attending a course, being lectured by an expert or reading a book. Historically, a great deal of management development has been concerned with the transmission of information with little regard for its relevance, applicability or potential impact – that is, it has been generic rather than personal, directive rather than negotiated. What is clear is that successful leaders are very focused on their personal and professional learning and development and understand themselves as learners as much as leaders.

One way of trying to understand how leadership learning takes place is to return to the image of a mindscape or mental map – a conceptual framework. The purpose of leadership development is to increase the usefulness of the map by ensuring that it is an accurate depiction of the territory to be covered and is relevant to the individual. The usefulness of any map is determined partly by its scale and partly by the information it depicts (and how it is depicted). As leaders develop, so their personal mental maps become more sophisticated, more detailed and, often, more idiosyncratic.

At the early stages of leadership development an atlas might be appropriate. This will then be refined to a road map which, in turn, will be honed to an A–Z street plan. However, the best maps are those which draw on generic information and personalise it to suit a particular purpose at a particular time. Although the analogy can be pushed too far, it may be helpful to think of leadership learning as the process of creating personal meaning from a complex environment with multiple reference points so as to facilitate a journey.

If leadership learning is about the development and enrichment of personal maps, then the learning process is subject to a number of variables that can be best expressed as propositions:

- In order to create new knowledge leadership development has to recognise and respect prior knowledge.
- Experience, of itself, has only limited value unless it is mediated by reflection and so modifies knowledge and behaviour.
- Successful learning is a function of positive emotional engagement which will inform motivation and sustainability.
- All leadership learning will be processed through personal value systems which will determine significance, applicability and prioritisation.

For leadership learning to lead to attitudinal change, and so to significant behavioural change, all four factors have to be recognised and incorporated into any strategy. The absence of any one component will compromise the other three – for example, a lack of emotional engagement will severely inhibit learning from experience because it is the interpersonal and intrapersonal that actually allows us to make sense of our experiences. Equally, knowledge that is not applied to experience is impoverished, and the absence of values makes all learning, literally, pointless. To achieve this level of learning, a range of strategies need to be in place:

- The development of a range of cognitive skills: analysis, logic and data interpretation.
- Learning activities which are based on problem solving in real-life situations.

- Reflection on actual experience based on appropriate feedback.
- Challenge derived from new ideas, confronting performance and so on.
- Coaching to help mediate the perceived gap between actual and desired performance.
- A sense of moral purpose, a vocation or a search for personal authenticity.

In practical terms, the most powerful basis for profound learning is supported reflection – support being provided through coaching and mentoring, the use of a reflective journal, structured reading to inform review and, perhaps most importantly, peer review and feedback on actual practice. Effective leadership development provides a sophisticated conceptual framework to support review, a systematic review process and support for analysis and action planning. However, leadership development is often an event rather than a process. Although it can model excellent practice, it needs to be part of a personal developmental process – such development is axiomatic to the leadership role. Perhaps one of the most significant aspects of this process is the recognition that learning is a fundamental component of the job itself, not an adjunct or a bonus. It is well known that leadership development, especially for head teachers, is the first casualty of any constraint on resources – time or money. This is not to argue for more time to be spent on courses but rather for the principles outlined above to become implicit to personal working patterns. For example:

- Building review into meetings and all individual and team projects.
- Scheduling time and space for regular reflection and creative thinking.
- Establishing a structured and regular pattern of professional reading and creating opportunities to discuss and apply insights gained.
- Regular meetings with a coach and/or mentor as part of a sustained (and sustaining) developmental relationship.
- Acting as a coach/mentor to others.

- Creating networks (virtual and actual) to nourish, support and challenge.

> Review, reflection and evaluation were once described as the Achilles heel of educational leadership. Would you accept this judgement in terms of your working practices?
>
> How could you protect your time as a leader to engage in these higher order working practices?

This first chapter has set out what we consider to be the framework for any discussion of leadership. The rest of the book is structured around seven key themes that we believe are the basis of contemporary school leadership. However, each of the seven topics is contentious and open to a wide array of interpretations and applications. We have provided a range of authoritative sources for each theme and identified important ideas, issues and debates. We have also provided a number of questions to stimulate thinking and serve as the basis of challenging underpinning assumptions and practices. We have not provided answers.

Why leadership?

Classify each of the following components of your leadership of change as A, B, C or D, according to the extent to which it shows:

A. High confidence and is well established in principle and practice.

B. Emergent practice for some of the time.

C. Some awareness but no consistent practice.

D. No awareness.

Leadership behaviours	**Rating/ evidence**	**Implications/ action**
In my school leadership is understood as collective capacity rather than personal status		
My leadership is distributed and inclusive rather than hierarchical and personal		
I place as much significance on developing followership as I do on leadership		
I am sensitive to cultural and gender-related issues in leadership practice		
'Leadership can be learnt' is a fundamental principle of my approach to leadership, and I devote time to my leadership development		
I can demonstrate how my leadership makes a difference		

Leadership behaviours	Rating/ evidence	Implications/ action
I have a very clear understanding of how my professional accountability works		
I am constantly reviewing, debating and updating my personal leadership mindscape		

Chapter 2

Creating a preferred future – leading change

There is a very strong case for arguing that one way of cutting the Gordian knot of the debate about the nature and components of effective leadership is simply to assert that leadership is primarily about change. This chapter focuses on the issues involved in leading change and explores the following specific areas:

- What are the main justifications for change in education?
- What are the issues in moving from improving to transforming?
- How much change is actually required?
- How can we create a culture of aspiration and hope?
- What is the role of strategic conversations and developing scenarios in leading change?
- How do effective leaders secure successful change and innovation?

Leadership and change

A key justification for the focus on leadership is that we have to change – stasis is rarely an option. The moral, relational and strategic imperatives usually associated with leadership are, in effect, dimensions of change. This raises the interesting possibility that the frequently used phrase, 'the management of change', may, in fact, be oxymoronic. It is possible to manage elements of the change process but not the actual process itself – that is far too complex for an operational perspective expressed through managerial solutions and fixes. Engaging with change requires the positive interaction of the components of leadership discussed in Chapter 1.

Popular discourse about change generally reflects two perspectives: firstly, change as an event to be managed and, secondly, change as a fundamental component of the human experience – change as a continuing and inevitable process. There now seems to be a broad consensus that change cannot be viewed as a sequence of events with each one being managed discretely. If important concepts such as improvement and transformation are seen as central to the work of leaders, then change is the core leadership process. It would be wrong to confuse successful project management with the leadership of change.

From a historical perspective, change seems to be a deep and abiding component of social institutions – from empires to football clubs there seems to be an almost organic cycle of growth and decay, rise and decline. For many involved in education, the change process does seem to be particularly challenging with frequent calls for a moratorium on change – which is rather like asking for a rest from having to breathe all the time. What is intriguing is the extent to which change is seen as problematic in education when the core process of education, learning, is, by definition, a change process. We learn because we change and as we learn so we change – neurologically, psychologically and socially. In many ways, the assessment of learning is about measuring the success of change processes.

How do you perceive change – as a sequence of events, the result of external imposition or a natural, organic process?

How is your perception reflected in the culture of your school?

Do you feel there is a resistance to change in your school? Is this culture based on fear, bad experiences or both?

Why change?

We expect leaders to bring about change – to enhance a football club's performance, to improve a school, to save the nation. In terms of leadership strategies, the implications of these expectations were first conceptualised by Charles Handy in the model of the sigmoid curve, as depicted in Figure 2.1. The rationale that underpins this model is that any human endeavour grows, waxes and then wanes. From the Roman Empire to former Premiership football clubs, from apparent permanent fixtures on the high street (e.g. Woolworths) to cities (e.g. Detroit), there are countless examples of the mighty falling. Woolworths, for example, failed to respond to the challenge of emerging competition from other budget outlets such as Poundland and Wilko. Even achieving eponymous status is no guarantee of survival – Kodak's refusal to accept the growth of digital photography is a classic example of almost wilful self-destruction.

Another way of understanding this phenomenon is to reflect on the extent to which we are seeking to improve what are essentially analogue schools in what is an increasingly digital age. Detroit was so fixated on being 'Motown' that it failed to recognise the danger signs of a changing economy. From a population of nearly 2 million at the peak of its success, Detroit now has less than 700,000 inhabitants and is bankrupt to the tune of US$18–20 million.

There are few examples of social organisations that demonstrate sustained growth over an extended period. Handy's key insight is that the function of leadership is to anticipate the downward curve and intervene in order to defer the inevitable decline.

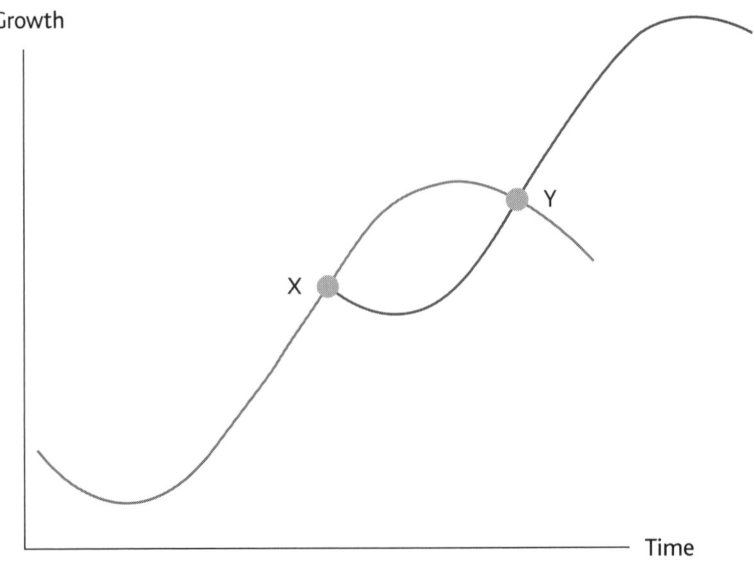

Figure 2.1. The sigmoid curve

At point *x*, when performance is improving, leaders need to focus on engaging with what Handy calls the 'second curve', before the onset of diminishing returns at point *y*:

> The message of the Second Curve is that to move forward in many areas of life it is sometimes necessary to change radically, to start a new course that will be different from the existing one, often requiring a whole new way of looking at familiar problems. (Handy 2015: 27)

If an organisation has reached point *y* then it is probably too late – decline is inexorable. This is the stage when the traditional strategies of school improvement may no longer be valid and a radical reconfiguration is required. The challenge of the sigmoid curve is that leaders have to initiate change while the prevailing orthodoxy is still working and by most criteria, save one, both appropriate and effective. The one criterion that is not being met is that current ways of working will almost inevitably lead to a period of diminishing returns when rising input does not lead to commensurate returns. There is also a very real danger of what might be termed 'leadership myopia' where more time is spent on short-term operational issues than long-term strategic thinking. In their study of school leadership commissioned by the Department for Education and Skills, PricewaterhouseCoopers offered the following analysis:

> Many head teachers recognise themselves that they are struggling to create sufficient time to engage effectively in the various strategic issues they are required to deal with. Part of this is driven by the sheer volume of operational delivery issues that school leaders now have to address. ...
>
> But these ties to the operational space also seem to be related, based on our interpretation of the evidence, to a mindset amongst some school leaders which is often more comfortable with an operational than a strategic role. (PricewaterhouseCoopers 2007: 5–6)

Underpinning this model of second curve thinking is the notion of prevention rather than cure, of moving from finding and fixing to predicting and preventing – that is, actively engaging with the future rather than passively acquiescing to external forces. Effective leadership identifies or anticipates key issues at point x on the diagram rather than hoping to put things right at point y. This implies a predisposition towards the strategic rather than the operational, and the importance of distinguishing between tasks that are appropriate to leadership and those that are broadly managerial in nature and outcome. It might even be appropriate to use that most reviled concept, proactivity, as a central element in our understanding of effective leadership and governance. Essentially, anticipation is better than reaction.

> Do you accept the sigmoid curve as a possible model to demonstrate change in education?
>
> Would it be appropriate to argue that educational policy in England has been, in effect, first curve thinking rather than second curve thinking? What opportunities are there for second curve thinking in your school?
>
> What are the implications of the model for the strategic thinking of school leaders, governors and trustees?

Another relevant concept that supports the idea of second curve thinking is predict and prevent, which is essentially a more robust version of 'prevention is better than cure'. It involves moving the culture of a team or school away from reaction to anticipation and intervention – crucially, the willingness to take action to prevent failure or enhance the potential for success. There are numerous examples of this approach from everyday life: the best way to avoid a heart attack is to stop smoking and not to invest in more cardiac surgeons, or the most effective way to maintain your car's efficiency is to have it regularly serviced. The best way to secure equity in education is to stop children failing because of the way the education system is designed.

In an education system that has been under almost continual pressure to improve and has been subject to a wide range of often contradictory policy initiatives, it is vital that leaders are able to provide a compelling justification for any proposed innovation or initiative. Howard Gardner provides the most basic rationale for change – when something no longer works or it is no longer relevant or appropriate.

> I discern two legitimate reasons for undertaking new educational practices. The first reason is that current practices are not actually working. ...
>
> The second reason is that conditions in the world are changing significantly. Consequent on these changes, certain goals, capacities, and practices might no longer be indicated, or even come to be seen as counterproductive. (Gardner 2006: 10)

If Gardner's criteria are applied to existing education policy in England, then it might be argued that the current school improvement strategy works very well in some contexts, but by no means all, and that the prevailing orthodoxies need to be questioned and tested as to the extent to which they are actually making an impact. As will be demonstrated in Chapter 4, current policies are not actually working in terms of securing equity – or, to be fair, they are working but at such a slow rate that it might take a generation before we see any real impact on society. Gardner's second critique refers to changes in the context of education – in essence, is the prevailing policy model fit for purpose?

There is a third rationale for engaging in a change process, which is that there might be a better way – that is, research or innovative practice offers an alternative way of working that appears to be vindicated by the available evidence. For example, research by the Sutton Trust into the deployment of teachers demonstrates the positive impact on the progress of the most disadvantaged and vulnerable pupils of being taught by the most effective teachers (Higgins et al. 2011). For many educators this seems to be counterintuitive; obviously, the best teachers go with the most able pupils, especially in a time of high stakes performance-based accountability.

Which of the following do you find the most compelling argument for change?

- Current practices are not actually working.
- A changing context means that the prevailing orthodoxy is counterproductive.
- Research indicates that there are more effective ways of working.

How might your preferred approach influence your leadership style?

Degrees of change

There are, of course, degrees of change (see Table 2.1). Some change is essentially cosmetic, some profoundly transformative. It is worth interrogating the extent to which the level of change is determined by actual necessity or by collective comfort with the status quo. Shallow or cosmetic change is basically about incremental adjustment and maintenance. As Handy's sigmoid curve implies, securing the long-term viability of an organisation may require radical rethinking of some basic assumptions and a significant change of direction and/or a refocusing of priorities – in other words, transformation. The most powerful metaphor for transformational change is probably the transition from caterpillar to butterfly. It is worth remembering that this type of change involves metamorphosis – the disappearance of the caterpillar to enable the emergence of the butterfly.

Shallow change – improvement planning	Cosmetic updating, 'tidying the garden', incremental improvement.
Deep change – innovation	A significant shift in an aspect of the school's working (e.g. academisation, joining a trust, changes in curriculum and assessment models).
Profound change – second curve thinking	A basic rethinking of established patterns of working, 'from caterpillar to butterfly' (e.g. personalising learning, a skills/topic-based curriculum).

Table 2.1. Degrees of change

The challenge for school leaders is the confidence with which they are able to determine the level of change that is necessary in their school. Is it a matter of nurturing and maintaining generally effective policies and processes, or is there a need for radical intervention to secure consistent quality in teaching and learning? Or does the system require a fundamental rethink?

The issue for education systems in many developed countries is not so much that they are not working – most of them demonstrate long-term incremental improvement (albeit very inconsistently) – and many children enjoy high quality teaching and learning, but rarely all the children all the time. The problem for leaders and policymakers is twofold: firstly, there are a significant number of young people who are not benefitting from the system and, secondly, the education that is being improved may not be relevant or appropriate to the 21st century. A good example of the implications of this type of thinking is the recent decision in Finland to abandon teaching cursive script (O'Connor 2015) and to move towards a curriculum that is presented thematically rather than as an aggregation of subjects (Garner 2015). This is classic second curve thinking, justified in terms of the impact of information technology and the need to prepare students for higher education and employment.

Is shallow change/incremental improvement enough, or do we need to explore deep and profound change?

Perceptions about the need for change are necessarily subjective. How would you assess the range of perceptions of your leadership team?

As a hypothetical exercise, it might be argued that the following issues could represent a second curve thinking agenda for many educational systems. In other words, they are unlikely to be achieved by even conscientious and diligent incremental improvement.

- Developing authentic equity and inclusion so that the disadvantaged and vulnerable are in no way systemically disadvantaged and forced to compensate for an increasingly polarised society.
- Moving towards the personalisation of learning, which is rooted in respect for the dignity and uniqueness of every learner, and securing consistently excellent teaching and learning, irrespective of context.
- Developing the school as a learning community that is designed as a key element in community renewal and building a democratic society.
- Collaborative working between schools becoming the norm with a genuinely school-driven education system.
- Building partnerships with communities and agencies so that parents and the wider community are fully equal partners in education.
- Working towards education for sustainability and recognising the issues emerging from climate change.

It seems to be the case that on certain important issues a graduated or incremental approach is appropriate and can work but it may take a very long time, and in the short to medium term it can make virtually no difference. For example, the gap between men and women's pay for full-time workers was 9.4 per cent in April 2015, compared with 9.6 per cent in 2014. While that was the narrowest difference since the figures were first published in 1997, there has been little change in the ratio overall. On that basis, according to the TUC, it will take almost 50 years to achieve pay parity between men and women (see Milligan 2015). This means that a further two generations of women will be subject to institutionalised discrimination. Women's pay has improved but the gender gap remains effectively the same. This reinforces a fundamental issue in the nature of any society, which is the extent to which the rhetoric of equality and equity is matched by interventionist strategies to close the gap and secure social justice for the current generation, rather than be content with the hypothetical possibility of success at some time in the future.

The issues around an incremental approach generate another concern about the extent to which a proposed change is within existing boundaries or horizons or seeks to redefine those boundaries. However, what is clear is that as the potential to challenge the status quo increases, so too does the potential for turbulence.

The more radical the change, the greater will be the potential for resistance or rejection and so the greater the challenge for leadership. For example, it might be argued that all of the work on the improvement of primary schools would have been better invested, according to the evidence (e.g. Desforges 2004), in improving the quality of family life, notably in terms of literacy and engagement in learning. To put it simplistically, working to improve the quality of family life might have had a greater impact on educational outcomes than working to improve schools. It might be that to secure literate children, what is required is a major focus on adult literacy. Furthermore, this has enormous potential collateral benefits. At present, according to the Literacy Trust, 16 per cent of adults (5.2 million) are functionally illiterate and 1.7 million adults have literacy levels below those expected of an 11-year-old.*

An example of second curve thinking is provided by Gompertz (2015: 193), who claims that 'All schools should be art schools'. This view would imply that:

> a more student-focused approach might now be feasible in our digital age. Could we not start to build a semi-bespoke curriculum tailored to the needs and interests of individual students? ...
>
> How viable is the one-size-fits-all model for a generation of students who have grown up using technology to curate their lives and interests? By the time many of them arrive at senior school they have

* See http://www.literacytrust.org.uk/adult_literacy/illiterate_adults_in_england.

> already personalized their world with playlists, Facebook homepages and Google filters.

This perspective is reinforced by Jukes and his colleagues (2010: 41):

> Today's children are experiencing a digital world that is increasingly, and some would even say completely, out of sync with traditional approaches and assumptions about teaching, learning and assessment ... our instruction is targeted at students from another age.

In some respects, we may already be on the downward slope of the sigmoid curve and therefore the need for second curve thinking becomes even greater. Further examples of second curve thinking might include:

- Scrapping GCSEs – virtually no other country places as much emphasis on tests at 16 as England and Ireland. It seems an unnecessary intervention when education now continues to 18.
- Working towards a system based on stage not age – questioning the arbitrariness of automatic chronological cohort progression and personalising education to recognise and respect the very real differences between learners.
- Developing a strategy for education that integrates educational provision from birth to 25 and beyond, or at least cradle to mortgage.
- Moving from teaching subjects to learning through themes (i.e. a more integrated and holistic approach that recognises how learning takes place in the workplace).
- Recognising the full potential of IT in securing educational equity – for example, the work of Dr Sugata Mitra (www.hole-in-the-wall.com).

What are the most radical scenarios that you would propose for the future direction of education policy?

From a moral perspective, what do you see as the most urgent priorities across the education system?

How do your pupils and their parents see the ideal future? How about the staff of your school, the governing body, your leadership team?

The nature of the change process

The most compelling motivation to change is not the implementation of external requirements, but rather the need to enhance our potential as human beings and our sense of moral commitment in order to contribute to achieving a desired future. This requires a movement away from authoritarian dogma underpinned by a power-coercive model to a world of authoritative evidence rooted in common values and mutual respect.

The starting point for any change process has to be the willingness of leaders to engage with change at a personal level, prior to seeking to secure change in others and the organisation – as Mahatma Gandhi is reputed to have said, 'Be the change you wish to see in the world'. What is increasingly clear is that people are not motivated and engaged by approaches based on essentially arbitrary rewards and punishments or threats and promises. Instead:

> The science shows us that the secret to high performance (is) ... our deep-seated desire to direct our own lives, to extend and expand our abilities, and to live a life of purpose. (Pink 2009: 145)

What combination of the following factors best describes your emotional response to deep and profound change?

- The status quo in education is morally indefensible – change is a moral imperative.
- My primary role as a school leader is to implement government policy.
- It is wrong to experiment with children's life chances.
- I am at my best in innovative and entrepreneurial situations.
- I prefer to follow the proven success of others.
- Change is not an option – it is a moral obligation.

The complex interaction of public and private approaches to change and change strategies is what makes the successful leadership of change so challenging. A great deal of the literature on leading change has tended to focus on change as a public process, but it is worth speculating on the extent to which the successful leadership of change is more attributable to the private dimension – motivation, engagement, commitment and the emotional response to both what is being changed and the actual change process itself. A useful insight into this tension is provided by Linsky and Lawrence (2011: 7) who distinguish between the technical and affective issues when leading change:

> While *technical problems* may be very complex and critically important (like replacing a faulty heart valve during cardiac surgery), they have known solutions. They can be resolved through the application of authoritative expertise and through the organization's current values and ways of doing things.
>
> *Adaptive challenges* can only be addressed through changes in people's values, beliefs, habits, and loyalties. Making progress on them requires going far beyond any authoritative expertise.

Change is a subjective experience with multiple realities and alternative perceptions which question any notion of objectivity or talk of reality. Only rarely can we claim with total confidence that this particular proposition is right. There are very few technical problems and solutions available in education, although there is an increasing amount of evidence to reinforce and support certain key perspectives – for example, the work of the Sutton Trust–Education Endowment Foundation on the deployment of pupil premium funding and the characteristics of 'great teaching' (Higgins et al. 2011).

Figure 2.2 attempts to identify the four main variables and possible relationships involved in understanding the leadership of any change process. Each sector has validity in certain contexts but the effective leadership of change is probably to be found in the diagonal shaded rectangle. The effective leadership of change involves being able to move with confidence between the bottom left and top right quadrants, depending on the school context and the particular focus of any change initiative.

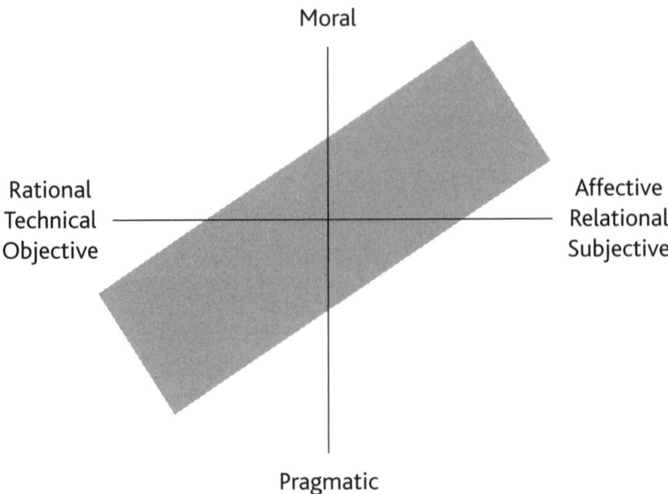

Figure 2.2. The alternative perspectives informing the leadership of change

In an ideal world, leaders would be able to move the diagonal rectangle so that it gradually occupies the top right quadrant – that is, the leadership of change is primarily understood in terms of moral and relational imperatives. However, the rational and pragmatic frames are necessary and appropriate at certain stages of leadership and organisational development, maturity and effectiveness. What might be seen as an immature culture will in time, hopefully, move into the more sophisticated and mature strategies and behaviours associated with occupying the top right-hand quadrant.

The four broad categories of possible approaches to leading change might be best understood in the following terms:

1. The moral imperative: This is very much related to the most basic understanding of leadership – that is, leadership is about 'doing the right things'. Consequently, in one sense, the imperative to 'close the gap' can be seen as essentially moral as it is concerned with securing equity across the system. In other words, change in education is social justice in action.

2. The pragmatic imperative: This is not so much cynical or realistic but rather an acknowledgement that, for the vast majority of educationalists, education is a public service funded through taxation

and therefore with commensurate accountability. In this context, most change initiatives are generated through external policies that are explicitly linked to funding and accountability. Thus, an approach to securing equity might be implemented through a system-wide strategy such as Every Child Matters. The ratio of externally generated change to local initiatives may be one of the significant factors in explaining the potential success or failure of a policy initiative.

3. Rational, technical, objective approaches: Very few human beings actually live a life planned out in detail in childhood. The world is too complex and there are too many intervening variables. But much management thinking is still posited on the rationalistic fallacy – the belief that the world is linear and predictable rather than complex and chaotic. The managerial approach often totally ignores the impact of ambiguous values and beliefs, organisational power politics and the multiple competing realities found in any human endeavour. If the world is understood as a complex adaptive system, then the leadership of change has to start from the premise that leadership strategies must be sensitive to that context and fit for purpose.

4. Affective, relational and subjective approaches: This is the perspective that dominates most human interactions. It is the world of feelings and relationships and it is the basis of how we make sense of our subjective experience of the world. This is the context where authentic collaboration, empathy, trust and a common language built around a shared sense of community become the key elements of any attempt to secure significant change. It may be that love and compassion are a more powerful motivator of change than a beautifully drawn Gantt chart.

Of course, these four elements do not exist in isolation from each other and the various permutations that are available reinforce the complexity of the leadership of change. Any model of leadership has to reflect the complex interaction of these variables which, in turn, will be significantly driven by the national policy context, the history of the school, the prevailing culture and ethos and morale in the school. In addition, the actual focus of any proposed change will be affected by another significant variable – fear of change. Most school leaders will have had the experience of underestimating the significance attached by staff to an apparently innocuous proposal to change what seemed to be a low significance and low status matter.

> Using the definitions provided to explain Figure 2.2, where would you locate some of the strategic decisions made by your leadership team in recent years?
>
> What are the implications of your findings for the policymaking process in your school?
>
> Is there anything in your personal and professional biography that supports the contention that the future can be predicted, that life follows a neat linear pattern and that we are in control of our destinies?

A further key variable influencing the nature of the change process is the extent to which the origin of any change to established patterns of working is internal or external to the school. This is simply a reflection of a basic human truth: successful personal change is the result of intrinsic motivation and a willingness to change. It would be naive to pretend that salaried professionals have anything like the personal autonomy that is often touted as a vital element of professional status. Equally, there is the fact that most education professionals work in the maintained sector which means they are using public funding – with all the accountability that this implies. However complex these relationships are in reality, Figure 2.3 is an attempt to represent the relationship and its implications.

Low engagement	→	**High engagement**
Externally imposed		Internally generated
Extrinsically driven		Intrinsic commitment
e.g. government policy		e.g. school-based innovation

Figure 2.3. Understanding the implications of origins of change initiatives

As might be expected, the degree of government direction, specification or outright control varies enormously. For example, there are many permutations of a range of variables that might explain the reasons for the sustained success of Finland's education system. Sahlberg offers the following analysis:

> A typical feature of education in Finland is the way teachers and students are encouraged to try new ideas and methods, learn from innovations and cultivate creativity in schools. At the same time, many teachers respect the traditions of good teaching. Education policies today are the result of three decades of systematic, mostly intentional development that has created a culture of diversity, trust and respect. (Sahlberg 2015: 177)

There is little doubt that an enabling, positive and high trust culture makes a substantial difference to the perceived significance of school-based change and innovation. However, it is worth reflecting on the fact that while the policy context for schools in England swings between high degrees of prescription and a laissez-faire approach, schools are remarkably distinctive and idiosyncratic in all sorts of ways.

Extrinsic imperatives to change are rarely as effective as personal motivation, and if they are implemented they are unlikely to secure full commitment and engagement. Any internet search focusing on the words 'leadership' and 'change' will produce dozens of strategies, toolkits, resources and techniques. No doubt many of them are useful in providing analytical structures and processes to support effective leadership, but of themselves they are no answer. In the final analysis, it appears that the successful leadership of change requires a balance of passionate commitment, moral imperatives and high quality relationships.

What is the balance between school-based innovation and externally imposed change in your school?

How do you regard creativity and entrepreneurship across the school's leaders, governors and trustees? Are they qualities you look for in terms of leadership and governance?

What needs to be changed?

In any discussion on the need for change, the priorities concerning what should be changed and the way in which change should be introduced, there is an obvious need to identify what might be called a strategic agenda – that is, the long-term priorities for the school, trust or system. Although most of the items on such an agenda will be generic across the system, there will always be issues that are specific to a particular time or place. A generic agenda for schools in England might include the following items:

- The need for a sustained focus on closing the gap but recognising that equity in education is increasingly elusive. The 50:30:20 rule still applies – family, community, poverty and social class can outweigh school effects.
- In the future, school improvement will be driven by autonomous schools collaborating (the self-improving school system) with system leaders working across partnerships, alliances, federations, trusts and chains.
- There will be opportunities for significant creativity in the curriculum and pedagogy in the context of very limiting assessment schemes.
- Economic constraints in the public sector will continue (assuming no further major economic crises), so education budgets cannot be guaranteed indefinitely. There will be an emphasis on high impact, high leverage strategies (i.e. more for less).
- Neoliberal approaches will become the dominant philosophy – market forces will prevail, there will be increasing privatisation and multiple providers of schooling. The role of the public sector will continue to decline, so there will be opportunities for alternative sources of provision, commercial involvement and social entrepreneurship.
- Education policy will be largely laissez-faire but with very tight performance-based accountability centred on a very limited notion of educational outcomes.

- Traditional employment patterns will gradually disappear (apart from in the public sector) – there will be more part-time, job share and short-term employment across trusts.
- Information technology will become increasingly powerful and cheaper, changing the ways in which information is accessed, how it is managed and how understanding is assessed.
- Climate change will become increasingly significant as a result of changes in weather patterns having an ever more dramatic impact on people's lives.
- Safeguarding and combatting extremism will be a high priority for schools.

Each of these areas will, in turn, have a far more detailed range of specific issues associated with them. For example, the first issue listed above, closing the gap, will have a range of short and medium term issues associated with it, such as:

- Securing and retaining highly skilled teachers to work with the most disadvantaged pupils.
- Maximising the impact of the pupil premium.
- Developing collaborative strategies across trusts and clusters of schools.
- Engaging with families.
- Developing integrated strategies with other agencies.

The nature of this list will be influenced by the context of a school, its historical policies and what it perceives to be its moral, educational and social priorities.

> To what extent is futures thinking a key element of your personal leadership approach?
>
> What is the quality of strategic thinking across your school?
>
> Are pupils, parents, staff, governors and members of the wider community involved in strategic conversations?
>
> Is there a place for what might be described as 'utopian thinking' in developing scenarios for the future of your school?

Securing equity and closing the gap pose major challenges to the dominant consensus about school improvement. In fact, these issues may not be resolved by focusing on schools alone – families, communities and the negative impact of social class and poverty need to be added to the equation. However, there is a further complicating factor in that, even if the gap is closed, schools may not be providing an education that is appropriate to a very rapidly changing world. Two insights from Gardner help to illuminate this perspective. Firstly:

> Those at the workplace are charged with selecting individuals who appear to possess the right kinds of knowledge, skills, minds – in my terms they should be searching for individuals who possess disciplined, synthesizing, creating, respectful and ethical minds. (Gardner 2006: 9)

This is an argument for education as a holistic and humanistic experience. This recognises that academic knowledge is important, but so too is the ability to make sense of that knowledge, to make connections, to open alternative perspectives, to be aware of the importance of relationships and to appreciate that learning can never be morally neutral.

Secondly, Gardner goes on to argue that the need for a good memory has been supplanted by the 'ability to survey huge bodies of information – print and electronic' and that the need 'to organize that information in useful ways looms more important than ever' (ibid.: 11).

Education is both a product and a determinant of the society it serves. Whatever its faults and shortcomings, the English education system has come a long way from the assumptions about gender, race, class and disability that determined the nature of education in the 19th century and also for much of the 20th century. In exactly the same way that what was considered appropriate 150 years ago is now seen as morally and socially indefensible, so there are changes in our current situation that point to the need for a fundamental rethink of how we perceive the nature of education, the role of teachers and schools and what constitutes an appropriate curriculum.

It was once considered a necessary accomplishment for the learner to be able to make their own pen, using a penknife to cut a quill to make a nib. Today, the quill, the ink and the knife do not figure in education – two have been superseded and one is now illegal. The quill has been replaced by the fountain pen, the ballpoint pen and now, in Finland at least, with skills on the QWERTY keyboard.

> Based on your own experience of leading change and being involved in change in education, what do you see as the most significant factors in the successful leadership of change and the most significant factors in blocking change?
>
> What, in your experience, are the elements that help to reinforce the positive and minimise the negative?

Leading change through quality relationships and collaboration

People will change because they see the change as reinforcing their personal beliefs, or because they see potential personal advantage in the change, or because they are committed to the person leading the change. Organisational change does not happen without significant personal change, and personal change is usually the product of highly effective personal relationships. There are numerous formulations for quality personal relationships, but trust seems to be the superordinate human quality and represents the quintessential need to move from individual skills and characteristics to a culture based on shared personal qualities – in other words, the movement from emotional intelligence (a personal capacity) to emotional literacy (shared potential). Trust is essentially an indication of interdependence and mutual commitment.

Clearly, the building of trust is a cumulative process, and this again reinforces the importance of leaders modelling trusting relationships alongside the actual change agenda. The rational and the affective have to be balanced and reconciled in order to enable people to adopt alternative ways of working and engaging.

> Do you recognise, and does your own experience either confirm or deny, the centrality of personal relationships in creating a culture that will enable effective change? What, from your experience, are the most significant personal qualities in securing consent and consensus around a proposed change?

The linking of leadership, change and collaboration can perhaps be best understood from two closely related perspectives: firstly, community as social capital (the quality of relationships) and, secondly, the potential for learning through community. It is worth highlighting how rarely personal and organisational change is seen as a learning process but, in fact, learning is all about change. One of the challenges of leading change is that it often involves unlearning and then relearning.

Hargreaves and colleagues, in their study *Performance Beyond Expectations*, identify collaboration and cooperation as fundamental to high performance:

> organisations that perform beyond expectations relate to their peers and even their opponents through creative and counter-intuitive combinations of competition and collaboration where success partly rests on the success of others and a sense of social justice inspires service to neighbours who are less fortunate. (Hargreaves et al. 2010: 58)

For most purposes, leading change almost always requires collaboration and cooperation. Although there will always be a place for the solitary hero-innovator, people need to come together to collaborate and cooperate in order to solve problems by initiating and enabling change that they are then committed to and so embed into their practice. Thus, the leadership of change can be understood as leadership that is working through shared learning.

It could be argued that, irrespective of context, culture or era, people spend most of their lives working with others to bring about change by solving problems of varying degrees of significance and complexity. There is a very high correlation between participation and commitment; the more involved I am, the greater the likelihood that I will become an advocate for the change. The more individuals feel a sense of ownership of the problem, the process adopted and the solution identified, the more likely they are to adopt the change and canvass for others to adopt it.

> Collaborative schools do better than individualistic ones. Within high schools, too, collaborative departments with strong professional communities perform more effectively than weaker ones. Although what counts as collaboration might vary, the overall evidence is consistent – teachers who work in professional cultures of collaboration tend to perform better than teachers who work alone. (Hargreaves and Fullan 2012: 112)

An alternative perspective, and a vindication of the principles outlined above is given by Saxenian (1996: 45) in her analysis of the reasons for the continuing success of Silicon Valley as the world centre of innovation and creativity:

> Silicon Valley's supportive social structures, institutions and collaborative practices provided a framework for mutual learning and adjustment. Thus, while competitive rivalries spurred technological advance among local producers, the regional economy was far from the simple free market of economic theory.

A key element in the culture of openness and sharing is the extent to which networking is seen as a necessary component of leadership. Leaders both model and enable the sharing of practice and ideas on a systematic basis with high status being given to networking activities.

> 'Collaborative schools do better than individualistic ones. Within high schools, too, collaborative departments with strong professional communities perform more effectively than weaker ones.' Do you agree with Hargreaves and Fullan?

The leadership of change in schools can lead to two highly dysfunctional outcomes. Firstly, the complexity of the change process, and sometimes the lack of skill and experience in leading change, can result in senior staff acting unilaterally 'to save time and get things done'. Secondly, the high stakes that can be associated with successful change in terms of influence and power mean that the leadership of change can degenerate into micro-political scheming and balkanisation on a par with an Italian Renaissance court where Machiavelli is the most appropriate guide. The antidote to these two potentially dystopian situations comes partly from creating a moral consensus and partly from building a sense of community based on a superordinate sense of shared purpose and endorsing strategies and processes focused on high quality relationships.

Two themes about the nature of the leadership of change are emerging from social neuroscience: firstly, that much of the motivation driving our social behaviour is governed by an overarching need to minimise threat and maximise reward and, secondly, that social experience draws upon the same brain networks to maximise reward and minimise threat as the brain networks used for primary survival needs. The successful leadership of change is principally about securing the commitment and engagement of all those involved, because people are predisposed to approach rather than avoid:

> engagement as a route to mastery is a powerful force in our personal lives. While complying can be an effective strategy for personal survival, it's a lousy one for personal fulfilment. Living a satisfying life requires more than simply meeting the demands of those in control. Yet in our offices and classrooms we have way too much compliance and way too little engagement. (Pink 2009: 112)

Rock (2008) has developed the SCARF model as a way of understanding our responses to different situations where people need to collaborate and be personally engaged. The model involves five variables that define our perceptions of social experiences – status, certainty, autonomy, relatedness and fairness – which inform and influence the extent to which we approach or engage with others or avoid engagement. When considering change, it is important for the leader to address human needs (and fears) in each of these areas. What impact will the change have on an individual's self-perception of each of these states? What will be their combined impact?

- Status: Status is about how we perceive ourselves in relation to others; high status makes us feel safe, low status leads to insecurity. *How might a proposed change influence perceived relative status?*
- Certainty: This is about the sense of control that creates confidence. We need to feel safe and that implies minimising ambiguity and the

unknown. *How far might a proposed change introduce uncertainty and ambiguity, thereby leading to a sense of a loss of control?*

- Autonomy: This is about the extent to which we are able to make meaningful choices from a range of valid options. *To what extent will a proposed change increase or diminish an individual's ability to make choices that influence his or her life?*
- Relatedness: Relatedness refers to the quality and quantity of our social networks – in essence, our sense of belonging. To a very significant extent we define ourselves in terms of our social relationships. *What possible effect will a proposed change have on an individual's social network and the quality of his or her relationships?*
- Fairness: We all seek balance and equity in our lives – it is the basis of much of our decision making. Children have a deep sense of what is and isn't fair. As adults we expect parity of esteem and consistency. *To what extent will the outcomes of the proposed change be fair and equitable?*

The successful leadership of change can be seen as a highly sophisticated recognition of the neurological basis of our social behaviour. Given that most people have a deep desire for a sense of control and continuity, this means that proposing change and encouraging innovation can be seen as prompting responses on a deeply neurological level. A recognition of the potential of change to stimulate primal responses is an essential pre-requisite to the successful leadership of change and innovation.

Do you have examples of a school-based change initiative being negative or counterproductive? If so, what were the defining characteristics of the situation, and what are the messages for leading change in the future?

Does the SCARF model help to explain the success or failure of a particular initiative and the behaviour of the key protagonists in the change process?

Strategies to support the leadership of change

The Checklist Manifesto by Atul Gawande (2009) is a study of failure and prevention. He worked as a surgeon and became increasingly concerned that so many patients seemed to suffer serious post-operative complications or die unexpectedly in the days following their operations. His analysis led to the conclusion that many of these problems were caused by operating staff failing to follow basic procedures. For example, a surgeon failing to wash his or her hands properly could cause an infection, or failing to account for all the swabs used in the process could lead to one being left inside the patient's body.

Gawande developed a 19-point checklist to be read out before and during each operation to ensure that all of the simple but vital procedures were followed. The outcome was a marked decrease (30 per cent) in the number of patients becoming seriously ill or dying after surgery. In his book, Gawande makes the distinction between errors of ignorance (mistakes we make because we don't know enough) and errors of ineptitude (mistakes we make because we don't make proper use of what we know). He writes that failure in the modern world is really about the second of these errors. He shows how the routine tasks of surgeons have now become so incredibly complicated that mistakes of one kind or another are virtually inevitable. It's just too easy for an otherwise competent doctor to miss a step, forget to ask a key question or, in the stress and pressure of the moment, to fail to plan properly for every eventuality. This is exactly the point about effective management: however inspirational a leader the surgeon is, hands must be washed and swabs counted!

The best way to close the gap in schools is to prevent children failing, and this means actively challenging poor and inappropriate performance. This, in turn, means identifying, defining and embedding appropriate performance. While there are a range of strategies and techniques that can help to manage the problem of variation, it is important that such interventions are reinforced and corroborated by a culture of prevention. In other words, it isn't just what we do, it's the way that we do it.

The theory of marginal gains was one of the philosophies that underpinned the extraordinary success of Team GB cyclists at the Beijing and

London Olympic Games and the Sky team at the 2012 Tour de France. When Sir Dave Brailsford became performance director of British Cycling, he set about breaking down winning a race into its component parts. His philosophy was simple: focus on improving a number of small things which would lead to a measureable improvement. Aggregating the gains then leads to cumulative incremental improvement which, in turn, is potentially transformational. Even an improvement of 0.1 of a second adds to the positive gain and increases advantage in an Olympic final.

Sir Dave believed that if it was possible to make a 1 per cent improvement in a whole host of areas, the cumulative gains would end up being highly significant and produce a marked advantage. He rigorously analysed all the potential weaknesses in the team's assumptions, policies and strategies, as well as all the latent problems embedded in habituated practice, so he could improve on each of them in order to maximise positive effects and minimise negative effects. For example:

- By experimenting in a wind tunnel, he noted that the bikes were not sufficiently aerodynamic.
- By analysing the mechanics area in the team truck, he discovered that dust was accumulating on the floor and undermining bike maintenance. He had the floor painted pristine white in order to spot any impurities.
- The team started to use antibacterial hand gel to cut down on infections.
- When he became general manager of Team Sky, he redesigned the team bus to improve comfort and recuperation.
- He probed deeper into untested assumptions, such as the dynamic relationship between the intensity of the warm-down and speed of recovery.

Each weakness, problem or negative factor was not a threat, but rather an opportunity to analyse the problem, make adaptations and so create marginal gains. The approach is fundamentally scientific in that it is objective, quantitative and draws conclusions from the testing and analysis of hypotheses. The potential impact of marginal gains in cycling are made even greater when the same principle is applied to personal skills and techniques.

It would be an interesting strategy to adopt a marginal gains philosophy across a school for staff and students. The culture this would create has very strong links to the idea of the growth mindset and lesson study – essentially a commitment to sustained improvement.

> Marginal gains may seem like an approach that only big corporations, governments and sports franchises can hope to adopt. After all, running controlled experiments requires expertise and, often, sizeable budgets. But a willingness to test assumptions is ultimately about a mindset. It is about intellectual honesty and a readiness to learn when one fails. Seen in this way, it is relevant to any business; in fact to almost any problem. (Syed 2015: 201)

A very small-scale example of the thinking underpinning predict and prevent and marginal gains is the issue of staff absence in the winter through illness – notably flu. Absences can both disrupt children's education and be very expensive in terms of cover. A preventative approach would be to offer all staff a flu vaccination – a cost of £8 per person at current prices. Another marginal gain could be achieved by the installation of antibacterial hand sanitisers in school that could help to limit the spread of winter viruses.

What aspects of school life are most likely to be amenable to interventions based on predict and prevent and marginal gains?

If change is regarded as a process that is symbiotic with learning and leadership, then it is imperative that key strategies to support change are rooted in successful learning. All change involves learning and relearning and is an essentially social process in which the personal capacity to learn and so change is a function of the quality and integrity of social relationships. One of the most compelling models that describes the relationship between change, collaboration and learning is Wenger's communities of practice. He suggests that:

> An organization's ability to deepen and renew its learning thus depends on fostering – or at the very least not impeding – the formation, development, and transformation of communities of practice, old and new. (Wenger 1998: 253)

According to Wenger's model, a community of practice is made up of three elements:

1. The domain: A shared area of interest that creates a commitment and a shared competence in working in that domain.

2. The community: In pursuing their interest in their domain, members engage in joint activities and discussions, help each other and share information. They build relationships that enable them to learn from each other.

3. The practice: Members of a community of practice are practitioners. They develop a shared repertoire (e.g. experiences, stories, tools, ways of addressing recurring problems) – in short, a shared practice.*

In the Wenger model, a professional learning environment is likely to foster a wide range of themes and topics (most of them focused on improvement, innovation and change) which are then developed through communities of practice. For example:

- The leadership team take it in turns to present a summary of recently published research or books and lead a discussion on possible implications for the school.
- A group of middle leaders are working on shared strategies to enhance their monitoring of teaching and learning.
- A number of communities of practice involving teachers and teaching assistants are focusing on strategies to support learning for understanding, using techniques such as action learning and lesson study.
- Pupils are being supported to work as communities of practice to explore the possibilities of personalising learning.
- Parents and governors are working to explore extending the school's engagement with the wider community.

A further powerful example of how collaboration can secure change through a learning process, and have a direct impact on school

---

* For more on Wenger's community of practice model visit: http://wenger-trayner.com/introduction-to-communities-of-practice/.

improvement, is Hargreaves' model of joint practice development. He describes joint practice development as the process by which:

> through mutual observation and coaching the donor reflects further on the practice that is being shared and explores ways in which it can be improved further. This is a process to which the recipient can also contribute as an act of reciprocity. In short, what begins as sharing practice ends up as a co-construction of practice that entails incremental innovation.
>
> The term that most accurately describes this process is joint practice development for it captures a process that is truly collaborative, not one-way; the practice is being improved, not just moved from one person or place to another. (Hargreaves 2011: 10)

Hargreaves also identifies what he calls 'the knowledge model of professional development', which is exemplified in courses that work on the 'expert-to-novice mode'. He argues that the practice model, which focuses on the 'progressive development of best practice', has made significant inroads into replacing this approach. The problem Hargreaves identifies with the practice model is that the sharing of good practice does not necessarily 'amount to practice transfer' – in other words, it makes limited impact on actual teaching and learning. He contends that joint practice development provides the answer to the problem of getting professional development to actually make a difference.

The power of Hargreaves' model is that it builds collaboration right into the improvement process – effective and high impact professional learning is rooted in a model of collaboration. This strengthens the case for collaboration in that it is not just structural but it is also embedded in learning and professional relationships, and so has a direct influence on the successful implementation of change.

Joint practice development is an important strategy because it puts individual teachers, working with colleagues, in charge of the change process. While this is not always possible, it does offer what is probably the optimal model in terms of embedding change that is most likely to have a direct and immediate impact on the quality of teaching and learning. If it is also supported by effective coaching, there is the real possibility of change initiatives actually making a difference in terms of both outcomes and processes.

There seems little doubt that joint practice development has the potential to be extended from classroom practice to leadership practice, and to make action learning the key process by which leadership processes and practices are improved and developed. The idea of middle and senior leadership team meetings having part of every agenda devoted to a form of joint practice review may be utopian, but it is exactly what Wenger describes as a community of practice. Essentially, it models the process for improvement in every aspect of the school's life.

A process that has helped schools engage with change and innovation is the 6 I's process developed by the Microsoft Innovative Schools Project.* This is made up of six chronological stages which, in turn, help to secure the integrity and rigour of the change and innovation process:

1. Introspection: preliminary analysis and review of the school's vision, identifying experience of involvement in the change process and successful application of models of learning.
2. Investigation: research to identify and evaluate what is already known and in use in the relevant area through benchmarking and identifying best practice.
3. Inclusion: developing high quality relationships and a culture of collaboration by bridging with the various stakeholder communities.
4. Innovation: identifying, generating and testing solutions in order to focus on optimum strategies.
5. Implementation: putting projects into practice, securing commitment and embedding change in all aspects of the school's practice and procedures.
6. Insight: review, reflection and evaluation to inform learning and planning of the next phase.

This approach provides a structure and coherence to the change process, while not replacing creativity and insight with bureaucratic controls and imperatives.

* See http://www.educatornetwork.com/schools.

Can you think of examples where a community of practice and joint practice development approach is most likely to facilitate change?

Can you see a place for a marginal gains approach in your change strategy?

When might you consider using the 6 I's approach?

Do these approaches recognise the complexity and potential ambiguity inherent in change processes?

The leadership of change is a complex, demanding and highly ambiguous aspect of leadership. The more educationally significant the change, the greater the potential for uncertainty, alternative perceptions, competing rationalities and abuses of power. In order to lead change, it does seem that school leaders need to develop a range of qualities that are not available through PowerPoint-driven training or off-the-shelf packages. These necessary qualities would seem to include:

- Moral confidence and professional courage.
- The ability to think strategically and engage with abstraction.
- High tolerance of ambiguity.
- Determination and resilience.
- High order social skills and emotional literacy.
- Personal authenticity and the ability to engender trust.
- Strategies for networking and building coalitions.
- Personal learning and growth.

Successful leadership of change is always context specific, with a range of complex and significant variables that are informed by the particular circumstances of the school. However, certain principles do seem to apply (albeit in varying degrees) to most change strategies in schools:

- There is a very clear understanding of the nature of the change in terms of prescription, resourcing, accountability and required outcomes.

- Leadership for change prioritises the moral and relational dimensions of the change process, notably trust.
- There is a clear rationale and justification for the change and it is recognised that change is a complex, messy process.
- Any particular change initiative is clearly set within a strategic view of the future of the school.
- The leadership of change is seen as a collaborative process that is open, democratic and inclusive.
- Successful change is most likely to be found in effective communities.

The wise leader recognises that their personal commitment to and enthusiasm for change may not necessarily be shared by all their colleagues. Significant change is rarely self-legitimating and almost never predictable, linear and rational. It is also worth stressing that change often involves loss, so one person's exciting innovation is another's sense of rejection. This is why change has to be seen as an essentially emotional process that requires shared learning across the community if it is to be embedded and implemented.

Creating a preferred future – leading change

Classify each of the following components of your leadership of change as A, B, C or D, according to the extent to which it is:

A. High confidence and is well established in principle and practice.

B. Emergent practice for some of the time.

C. Some awareness but no consistent practice.

D. No awareness.

Leadership behaviours	**Rating/ evidence**	**Implications/ action**
Confident understanding of the changing environment of education		
A strong sense of a preferred future and confidence in building alternative scenarios		
Seeing change as a moral act and based in evidence – a willingness to engage in second curve thinking and challenge the status quo		
Personal confidence in changing and leading change		
Recognising that change involves engaging with multiple perspectives and ambiguity – recognising change as an emotional experience		
Willingness to support innovation and empower others to lead change		
Awareness of techniques and strategies to support the change process		

Chapter 3

Leadership as a moral activity

Virtually every school leader we have ever worked with would accept Warren Bennis' proposition that leadership is about doing 'the right things'. The interesting and significant debate comes with reaching agreement on what the right things are. This chapter explores this aspect of leadership by focusing on the following questions:

- How successful is your leadership in creating a moral consensus across your school?
- Would you agree that securing equity is the central moral issue for school leaders?
- What is the relationship between personal and professional authenticity and integrity?
- How confident are you in your team's ability to take decisions that 'do the right things'?
- How do you help your senior and middle leaders to develop moral confidence?

As we argued in the previous chapter, there is a general consensus that the single biggest issue facing school leaders today is the fact that education in England is primarily characterised by a deeply embedded and systemic lack of equity. Although, by a range of measures, there is equality in terms of the entitlement to be educated, there is, in contrast, a real lack of equity across the system. In other words, every child has the right to go to school (and this is a precious right) but not every child goes to a good school (and that is a moral issue).

Even in good schools there is often a lack of equity – there can be real variation in the quality of teaching and learning. Equally, although there has been a focus on school improvement that has made a very real difference in terms of overall performance, we have not yet closed the gap in terms of structural disadvantage. In economic terms everybody is better off, but the gap between rich and poor remains stubbornly wide. In educational terms we need to move from generic school improvement towards targeted interventions that support the learning of the most vulnerable.

> There is a growing body of evidence that shows that the highest performing education systems are those that combine equity and quality. Equity in education is obtained when personal or social circumstances, such as gender, ethnic origin or family background, do not hinder achieving educational potential (fairness) and all individuals reach at least a basic minimum level of skills. (OECD 2015: 31)

There seems little doubt that much of the explanation for the lack of equity lies in social factors, deeply entrenched child poverty, issues around parenting and the quality of community life, and the continuing negative impact of social class on British society. However, a significant proportion of the variables influencing equity are directly related to school leadership, and one of the most significant of those – the values that inform leadership – is the focus of this chapter. It seems to be the case that getting leadership right is the essential precursor to translating ethical precepts into practical action.

To what extent do you perceive your role in moral terms?

Is there any significant difference between doing the job well and being morally motivated and having a sense of vocation?

Is there an alternative perspective to equity in terms of a moral perspective for school leaders?

What are the right things?

Greene (2013: 258) offers the following scenario (based on Peter Singer's (1972) example of the drowning child):

> Suppose that you're out for a stroll in the park when you encounter a young child drowning in a shallow pond. You could easily wade in and save this child's life, but if you do, you will ruin your new Italian suit which cost more than $500. Is it morally acceptable to let this child drown in order to save your suit? Clearly not, we say. That would be morally monstrous. But why is it morally acceptable for you to spend $500 on a suit if you could instead use that money to save a child's life by making a donation to an international aid organization?

The obvious point here is that personal moral judgements are a matter of balancing a range of imperatives and perceptions. As Greene goes on to point out, if saving the drowning child is a moral imperative, then why is saving the starving child morally optional? There are obvious issues of immediacy and proximity but the problem is a real one: where are the boundaries to moral responsibility, and what are the limits to commitment? This has fundamental implications for effective leadership. In essence, it is about moving beyond the historical boundaries of the school as an autonomous institution into a recognition of the far wider moral responsibility in which the pursuit of equity transcends parochial interests. In the current climate in England, this degree of altruism may be very challenging:

> The hardest part of sustainable leadership is the part that provokes us to think beyond our own schools and ourselves. It is the part that calls us to serve the public good of all people's children within and beyond our community and not only the private interests of those who subscribe to our own institution ... Sustainable leadership is socially just leadership. (Hargreaves and Fink 2006: 158)

Do you agree with Hargreaves and Fink that there is a moral imperative to serve 'the public good of all people's children' and not just those who attend your school?

Where does this proposition potentially take our understanding of effective leadership?

One way of approaching the issue of what constitutes 'the right things' is to adopt a rigorous approach based on the concept of effective altruism. MacAskill suggests that altruism – the recognition of the rights and needs of others and the willingness to act on that recognition – is an essential component of any moral system. He challenges the purely emotional response to need and argues that what is required is effective altruism that will actually make a difference by:

> doing the most good with whatever resources you have. Importantly effective altruism is not just about making *a* difference, or doing *some* amount of good. It is about trying to make the *most* difference you can. (MacAskill 2015: 15)

This means taking a scientific, rational, impartial and evidence-based approach to making decisions about how best to support the needs of others. This clearly involves some kind of moral algorithm – a means of using data to make the most effective decision.

MacAskill illustrates this argument with an example that all teachers will recognise and empathise with, although it may not be directly transferable into the English education system. The example is taken from a charity working with schools in Kenya. The challenge was to improve school attendance. Various strategies were tried – new textbooks, extra teachers and the use of flipcharts – but the radical departure was the introduction of randomised controlled trials. Data was collected and rigorously analysed from schools using the new methods, while a control group did not use the new resources. None of the obvious strategies actually made any difference. What did make a difference was deworming – a simple, cheap treatment to remove intestinal worms that made children ill. Deworming reduced absenteeism by 25 per cent and children who had been treated spent an extra two weeks in school (MacAskill 2015: 11).

We often make our moral decisions on emotional grounds – the starving child, the horror of war, natural disasters. MacAskill suggests that we should be applying the test of effective altruism to any moral choice by asking five questions:

1. How many people benefit, and by how much?
2. Is this the most effective thing you can do?

3. Is this area neglected?
4. What would have happened otherwise?
5. What are the chances of success, and how good would success be?

With appropriate modifications to suit the context of the school, it is possible to see these questions being developed to serve as the basis of a careful analysis of the options and implications of choices in any leadership or governors' meeting where decisions are being made about the deployment of scarce resources. The example of the Kenyan schools that MacAskill uses provides a very powerful and corrective message to educational leaders: your natural instincts may not necessarily be the most appropriate source for authoritative decision making and 'the right thing' may not always be immediately obvious.

Goldacre makes the point that much of the opposition to the widespread use of randomised trials in medicine came from very senior practitioners who saw the evidence-based approach as a challenge to their authority, which was based on experience rather than a process developed from valid, reliable and trustworthy research. Is there the possibility that, in education too, decisions are taken on the basis of personal belief and experience rather than empirical and objective evidence?

> Where they are feasible, randomised trials are generally the most reliable tool we have for finding out which of two interventions works best. We simply take a group of children, or schools (or patients, or people); we split them into two groups at random; we give one intervention to one group, and the other intervention to the other group; then we measure how each group is doing, to see if one intervention achieved its supposed outcome any better.
>
> This is how medicines are tested, and in most circumstances it would be regarded as dangerous for anyone to use a treatment today, without ensuring that it had been shown to work well in a randomised trial. (Goldacre 2013: 8)

The growth in teaching school alliances, partnerships and academy trusts would seem to provide a golden opportunity to create a culture in schools that is research and evidence based. Such a move would provide an opportunity to create a new body of authoritative professional knowledge, increase confidence in the efficacy of interventions, and focus professional learning and development on real-time issues.

The common criticism of randomised controlled trials is that they experiment with people's lives and disadvantage the people in the control group. The second point is quickly dismissed as in such trials there is almost always a protocol that as soon as there is evidence that the desired outcome is being achieved then it should be made available to all. The first concern is also easily disposed of:

> To those who say it is unethical to 'experiment with people's lives' the proper response is that the alternative – failing to use the resources available to improve the lives of as many people as possible – is much worse. (Singer 2015: 156)

To what extent is your leadership evidence based?

Is there a research culture in your school where continuing professional development (CPD) as information transfer is being replaced by teacher-led research?

What protocols are in place to ensure that complex choices provide maximum benefit to the optimum number of learners?

Personal morality is very personal and subjective, but in practice we all live and work in a social context where our behaviour is defined partly by social norms and expectations and partly by the legal system. While the law is, at least in theory, objective (the speed limit is 30 mph, not 32 mph), morality is clearly far more subjective and open to interpretation. This is where leadership becomes significant. As we argued in Chapter 1, the articulation of an organisation or community's values is one of the defining responsibilities of leadership. Obviously, this is not a licence for the imposition of personal prejudices but rather about building a consensus based on informed consent. The starting point for successful leadership is clarity and confidence about personal values, as illustrated by Figure 3.1.

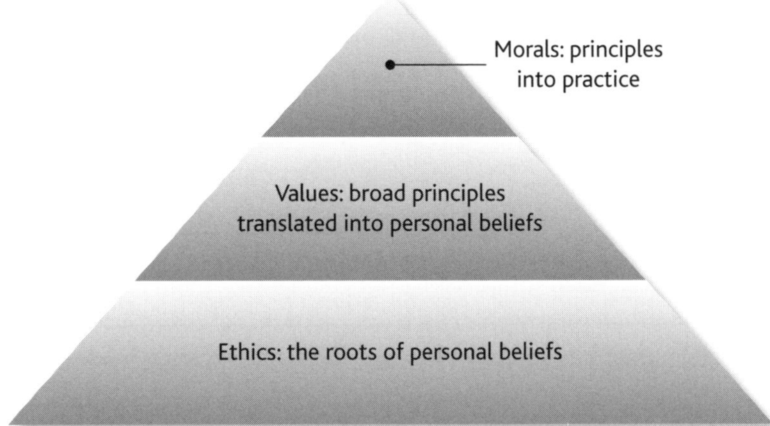

Figure 3.1. Developing moral confidence

Effective leadership emerges from a deep understanding of our ethics, values and morals. Leadership has to be deeply rooted in an ethical code – a clear framework that provides the foundations for personal and professional life. However, most ethical codes and philosophies are historical and generic and should only be applied at a particular time and place (i.e. contextualised into a personal values system). The effective leader thus takes a generic principle and translates it into a personal value that they can live by and that will inform their leadership decision taking. For example, although educators still believe in the importance of appropriate behaviour in school, they no longer accept that corporal punishment is an appropriate means of achieving it.

Values, however, have to operate in the real world and so they need to be translated into moral practices that inform day-to-day living. So, a school leader who is committed to social justice (ethical principle) translates that into a belief that a school has to respect diversity and be inclusive (personal and professional values), which is then reflected in school policies in a systematic and consistent manner (moral practice).

This is where school leaders need to create opportunities to spend time in conversation and in dialogue with colleagues and friends, and perhaps a coach, in order to refine, clarify and explore the implications of their personal values. It is not enough for leaders to articulate and canvass for certain principles – they have to embody them in their own lives and practice. In other words, they have to be authentic.

Authenticity is the result of the interaction of personal and professional values, the language adopted and the behaviours employed. Authenticity is the product of the consistency of beliefs, language and behaviour – walking the talk.

It might be an interesting exercise to take Figure 3.1 and complete it with your interpretation of each level, in terms of your personal ethical foundations and how they are translated into your values and day-to-day practice.

For example, how confident are you that your belief in the fundamental right of every child to excellent education is being met every day for every pupil? If your personal values are rooted in a belief in the importance of democracy, how genuinely democratic is your school?

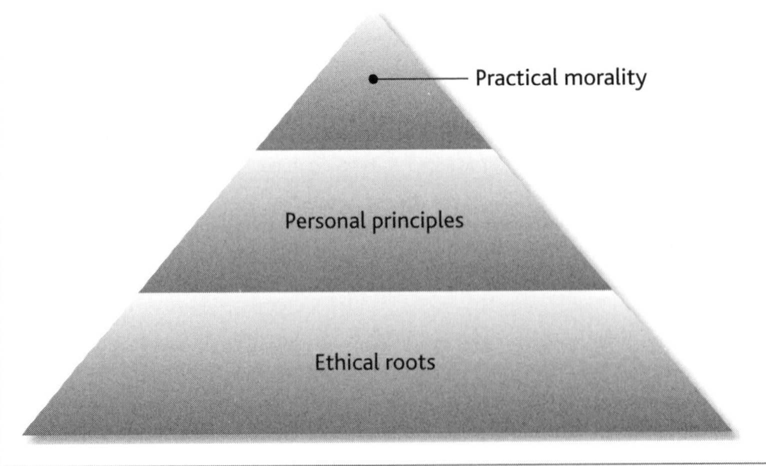

What is contentious in any debate about the role of values in society is the definition of the 'right things'. In one sense, they are the virtues that are implicit in leading a positive life in a modern democracy. The Ofsted *School Inspection Handbook* for September 2015 is very clear about core values:

> acceptance and engagement with the fundamental British values of democracy, the rule of law, individual liberty and mutual respect and

> tolerance of those with different faiths and beliefs; [students should] develop and demonstrate skills and attitudes that will allow them to participate fully in and contribute positively to life in modern Britain. (Ofsted 2015: 36)

Of course, these are not exclusively British values; at the least they are European values and probably universal human values.

One simple expression of the ethical basis of contemporary school leadership might be found in the formulation of the 3 E's – equity, excellence and effectiveness. These three principles would seem to be present in most of the great faiths and philosophies as well as being meaningful in modern democratic and secular societies. They are also consistently referred to, directly or indirectly, by educational policymakers; they appear, in a variety of guises, in the values or mission statements of most schools.

Equity, excellence and effectiveness would also seem to be appropriate in both the public and private sectors and across a range of social and cultural norms. Crucially, they probably reflect what most educationalists would accept as non-contentious principles that should inform their practice. As Greene observes:

> We can argue about rights and justice forever, but we are bound together by two more basic things. First, we are bound together by the ups and downs of the human experience. We all want to be happy. None of us wants to suffer. Second, we understand the Golden Rule and the idea of impartiality behind it. Put these two ideas together and we have a common currency, a system for making principled compromises. We can agree, over the objections of our tribal instincts, to do whatever works best, whatever makes us happiest overall. (Greene 2013: 351)

This is not to say that equity, excellence and effectiveness are unproblematic. There are enormous potential debates about their relative significance and the extent to which any one of them might be regarded as superordinate in a specific situation. However, the debate about their significance and the influence of contextual factors goes to the very heart of being a moral person, let alone a school leader. It is all about choices – what Greene refers to as 'principled compromises'.

On this basis, it is probably worth arguing that a combination of equity, excellence and effectiveness serves most perspectives in terms of the moral foundation of education. The 3 E's could therefore could be seen as a decent starting point for the suggestion that school leadership is essentially about securing social justice.

- Equity: It is not enough to simply ensure that every child goes to school. Every child has the right to go to a good school *and* have access to the most appropriate teaching and learning.
- Excellence: There has to be a commitment to ensuring that the school system operates to secure the optimum outcomes for every learner and that there is a clear understanding of the nature of excellent outcomes and strategies to ensure that all may access them.
- Effectiveness: Policies and human and physical resources are managed in such a way as to maximise their impact on the achievement of equity and excellence (i.e. the school keeps its promises).

So, it is not enough just to be equal. There also has to be parity in terms of the measureable outcomes of living in society:

> equity is not the same as equal opportunity. When practiced in the context of education, equity is focused on outcomes and results and is rooted in the recognition that because children have different needs and come from different circumstances, we cannot treat them all the same. (Noguera 2008: xxvii)

Social justice has to be impartial (the statue of Justice is traditionally depicted as being blind) and so it should be rooted in fairness. Nothing should compromise the essential parity that serves as the starting point for all social action. This raises the very challenging notion that in order to secure social justice, it may be necessary to discriminate in favour of certain groups – to misquote Aristotle, 'The greatest injustice is to treat everybody the same'. This is the principle underpinning the pupil premium and the recognition that special needs require special strategies. The central implication of this is that we may need to start thinking about school leadership as being focused primarily on securing social justice through the integration of equality and equity. Social justice only exists to the extent that the principle of equality is reflected in the actual concrete experience of all people found in any given social situation, and that experience has to be measured in the equity of outcomes. The more that equality and equity are integrated, the greater the level of social justice.

> How comfortable are you with the notion that your work as a school leader is primarily about the achievement of social justice?
>
> Does this perspective make any difference to your daily work pattern?
>
> Does a focus on social justice have implications for your work with other schools and the agencies responsible for the health and well-being of young people across your community?

The place of morality in school leadership

Barber et al. (2010: 5) capture the importance of the relationship between leadership, raising standards and closing the gap in the following synthesis:

> A major study of improving schools in England ... found that 'there are statistically significant empirical and qualitatively robust associations between heads' educational values, qualities, and their strategic actions and improvement in school conditions leading to improvements in student outcomes.'

As far as we are aware, there is no structured support or provision for potential and practising school leaders to spend time reflecting on their personal values and what might be called the morality of school leadership. Equally, there are limited opportunities to explore moral confidence – the courage to take the tough decisions and make the hard choices. Leadership, in almost any social context, can be seen as essentially concerned with making decisions and 'doing the right thing'. Leaders in education, from the classroom to the multi-academy trust, spend their working days making choices. Some choices are simple, of limited consequence and quickly forgotten in the complexity of daily life in schools. Other decisions are literally life changing, have profound implications for those affected and set precedents for years to come. The choices made by teachers in their classrooms are microcosms of the choices made by school and system leaders. The scope and scale of the decision is not the significant factor; rather, it is the integrity of the decision-making process.

Other professions provide some opportunities for leaders to explore the ethical foundations of their leadership. The British Army publishes *Values and Standards of the British Army*, which serves as an authoritative source of guidance on the principles and practice of all military personnel and, in particular, provides the conceptual framework for the rules of engagement that guide the strategy, tactics and operational decision making of all ranks. The General Medical Council publishes *Professional Values and Fitness to Practice* to guide the professional values of medical students, while the Medical Ethics Committee of the British Medical Association acts as an authoritative source of guidance and advice on ethical matters.

Except when things go very wrong, there are very few occasions when education professionals have the opportunity to review and reflect on their choices and so learn from them. This is very different to the supervision model found in social work, the clinical case review process found in medicine and the requirement for formal supervision for counsellors and psychotherapists. It is difficult to find any parallels to this kind of provision for the education profession.

A major gap in provision was identified following the financial crisis of 2007, where personal advantage, exploitation and a lack of any sense of accountability or social responsibility seemed to characterise certain elements of the business community – in particular the banking sector. Concern over the consequences of this gap, and anxieties that business school MBA graduates were seen as more concerned with profitability than social responsibility, led a Harvard Business School graduate to develop a code of ethics that was adopted by many of his colleagues and is now part of a movement found in over 250 business schools.* The essence of the oath is captured in the following summary:

> In exercising my professional duties according to these principles, I recognize that my behavior must set an example of integrity, eliciting trust and esteem from those I serve. I will remain accountable to my peers and to society for my actions and for upholding these standards.

Obviously, the swearing of the MBA Oath does not guarantee that the person taking the oath will actually follow its precepts; in exactly the same way as when doctors swore the Hippocratic Oath it did not

* For more information about the MBA Oath visit: http://mbaoath.org/.

preclude the possibility of inappropriate or incompetent practice. However, the MBA Oath and the Hippocratic Oath, in its modern variants, provide a conceptual framework to help define professional practice and create a shared vocabulary to enable professional dialogue.

> Do the *National Standards of Excellence for Headteachers* fulfil the same need as the Hippocratic Oath or the MBA Oath are intended to fulfil?
>
> Is there a case for school leaders taking a public oath on appointment?
>
> Does education need an ethics committee, or can we be confident about personal conscience and professional relationships being sufficient to ensure probity?

There is no doubt that there is a very powerful professional consensus that informs school leadership and that the personal integrity of school leaders is fundamental to the success of schools. But, in the current climate, there are more challenges than ever to any sense of professional hegemony. The day-to-day work of leaders is essentially about taking decisions and solving problems; leadership is a continuous process of exercising choices, all of which have moral implications. Marsh (2015: 83), in his account of his life as a neurosurgeon, captures these tensions:

> There was a slightly grim, exhilarating intensity to the work and I quickly lost the simple altruism I had as a medical student. It had been easy then to feel sympathy for patients because I was not responsible for what happened to them. But with responsibility comes fear of failure, and patients become a source of anxiety and stress as well as an occasional pride in success.

There are a range of potential moral dilemmas and emotional challenges facing school leaders – for example:

- The evidence that banding, streaming and setting are only of benefit to those students placed in higher groups – for the others the impact can be highly negative (Hallam and Parsons 2014).
- The need to deploy the most effective teachers with the most vulnerable learners if these pupils are to make progress and achieve (Higgins et al. 2011).

- The very clear evidence that certain teaching and learning strategies are more effective than others and therefore personal professional autonomy may be less significant than securing consistently high quality teaching and learning (Bloom 1984; Hattie 2009).
- The finding that leaders are at their optimum effectiveness when they are actively involved in, and give priority to, the learning and development of teachers (Robinson 2011).
- The most effective strategy for school improvement is for outstanding schools to support other schools (Desforges 2004).

> What is your emotional response to the tensions and dilemmas faced by school leaders? Do you recognise Marsh's reference to 'fear of failure' and 'a source of anxiety and stress'?
>
> What, from your perspective, should be the balance between values, evidence and practice?
>
> Are there occasions when a pragmatic approach is justified? What sort of precedents might this set?

There is no leadership decision-making process that does not have moral implications. Leadership can never be morally neutral; in fact, as was discussed in Chapter 1, Bennis and Nanus (1985: 21) argue that leadership is about 'doing the right things'. This implies that leadership should be rooted in an explicit ethical framework with consistent values that inform personal and professional behaviour. This would suggest that there is a correlation between an explicit, consensually based moral code and organisational success:

> The high quality and performance of Finland's educational system cannot be divorced from the clarity, characteristics of, and broad consensus about the country's broader social vision ... There is compelling clarity about and commitment to inclusive, equitable and innovative social values beyond as well as within the educational system. (Hargreaves et al. 2008: 80)

Finland provides a very interesting model of how an education system can be a product of the society it serves. Two key concepts, both derived from Lutheran theology and morality, help to explain why the exhortation from politicians to perform like Finland is fundamentally flawed.

Consensual authoritarianism and egalitarian conformity help to explain a society with a very high level of moral consensus and what might be best described as a practical morality. One expression of this is found in the Corruptions Perception Index which measures the relative levels of corporate corruption. In 2015, the countries with the highest scores, and lowest levels of corporate corruption, were:

1. Denmark
2. Finland
3. Sweden
4. New Zealand
5. Netherlands/Norway

Of the 168 countries surveyed the UK is tenth.*

Consensual authoritarianism can be best understood as hegemony across the community. In other words, it is the collective will that is expressed in the norms and expectations by which the community functions on a day-to-day basis. The community's norms are sufficiently strong to make deviation the exception. This approach is reinforced by egalitarian conformity which stresses the importance of avoiding extremes or polarisation in society. It seems to be the case that high performance requires, among many other things, a very strong moral consensus that is translated into what might be called practical ethics, which guide personal and organisational behaviour and decision taking.

Even if a long-term social consensus is not available, the deliberate and systematic adoption of a coherent and systematic moral code can have a significant impact on the life of a school and community:

> for the majority, the values based on the United Nations Convention on the Rights of the Child (CRC) and 'guide to life' provided by the RRSA (Rights Respecting School Award) has had a significant and positive influence on the school ethos, relationships, inclusivity, understanding of the wider world and the well-being of the school community, according to the adults and young people in the evaluation schools. (Sebba and Robinson 2010: 13)

* See http://www.transparency.org.

> What is the role of school leaders with regard to securing and embedding a social consensus around core values?
>
> Is it appropriate to see the school as a microcosm of society?

Principle into practice

Social justice requires the recognition and acceptance of diversity as a manifestation of equity and inclusion as a practical exemplification of equality. This is, in fact, a very complex process – leaders are judged by the extent to which they are able to translate principle into practice, dreams into reality and make hopes concrete. The challenge for educational leaders is to find strategies that combine the need for a critical and analytical perspective with the ability to inform actual practice. To extend Bennis' dictum, if leadership is about doing the right things, then it is not enough to debate the nature of the right things; an equal responsibility is to consider the means of securing the appropriate practice.

> The unity of a critical theory and a critical practice is not, therefore, the unity of a theory of education on the one side and a practice of criticism on the other. It is the unity of an educational theory with an educational practice ... The nature of educational values must be debated ... not only as a theoretical question, but as a practical question of finding forms of life that express them. (Carr and Kemmis 2006: 208–209)

This takes us to the key issue with translating principle into practice: it is not enough just to act; action has to be morally consistent and convert aspiration into actuality. In many ways, these principles provide a powerful and practical expression of any strategy to secure diversity:

> The heart of the school as a moral community is its covenant of shared values. This covenant provides the basis for determining its morality ... the virtuous school subscribes to and uses these moralities as a basis for deciding what its values are and how they will be pursued. (Sergiovanni 1992: 108)

This perspective on school leadership has very real implications for the place of values in education, particularly in a society that is increasingly heterogeneous, where achieving the well-being of all children is an elusive aspiration and where educational outcomes are highly variable. However, there are some very concrete ways in which schools can demonstrate a practical commitment to equity and social justice – for example:

- Schools as communities: The school works as an inclusive community that embodies diversity in its day-to-day working. It functions as a highly interdependent and interconnected network. Crucially, there is a culture of care and an acceptance of mutual responsibility for the well-being of all members of the community.
- Personalising learning: In order to ensure that equity and inclusion are directly expressed in the actual experience of students, the design of the curriculum and teaching and learning strategies are based around the needs of the student – the approach is à la carte, not table d'hôte.
- Student voice and leadership: It is not enough to assume that policies to respect diversity and enhance inclusion are working. There has to be systematic intelligence gathering to ensure that services are being provided on the clients' terms. This means giving students and other users the opportunity to voice their views about the quality of their experience and deliberately and systematically involving them in every aspect of planning for the provision of their services. In the final analysis, inclusion will only work if the students perceive themselves to be included.
- From 'find and fix' to 'predict and prevent': That prevention is better than cure is a well-known adage. Leadership for diversity and inclusion has to work from the premise of preventing discrimination and securing inclusion, rather than reacting to a lack of respect for diversity and a failure to be inclusive.
- Restorative justice: Respecting diversity and securing inclusion are not just policy issues, they are deeply personal and have highly emotional connotations. Restorative justice aims to ensure that a victim feels safe when challenging inappropriate behaviour and language. It should work to develop strategies that minimise the possibility of similar behaviour in the future.

These broad principles can be developed into more detailed and explicit criteria in order to review the extent to which a school is translating principle into practice and is embedding its policies and procedures – for example:

- There is an explicit commitment to values consistent with equity and inclusion and these are used to inform staff appointments, job descriptions, appraisals, CPD and all dimensions of the school's policies and strategies.
- Equity and inclusion are given appropriate status in terms of leadership responsibility and the deployment of senior staff.
- Governors regularly focus on equity and inclusion in their review and challenge processes.
- Pupil leadership is used to provide a contribution to the shaping of the school as a moral community focusing on the actual experience of learners. Pupil leaders are given specific duties with regard to the engagement of their most vulnerable peers.
- Pupil voice is used to review and evaluate the integrity of their learning experiences.
- The school is actively involved in projects and campaigns that support social justice in education (e.g. the work of UNICEF and the Co-operative Schools movement).
- Resources are deployed according to need (e.g. the most effective teachers work with the most vulnerable learners).
- The curriculum experience is personalised to maximise progress, engagement and the potential for success.
- Intervention strategies are used to anticipate and prevent failure.
- Financial and material resources are allocated on the basis of moral priorities.
- Senior leaders and governors use data-based and qualitative evidence to monitor and evaluate the appropriateness and impact of ameliorative strategies, and modify strategies appropriately.

> What is the relationship between principle and practice in your school?
>
> On the basis of the criteria set out above, to what extent is your school a community rooted in social justice?
>
> Is your school in a position to apply for the UNICEF Rights Respecting School Award?

When we consider the nature of social justice in education, there are two fundamental assertions to be considered. Firstly, social justice cannot be diluted, diminished or denied – either there is social justice or there is not. Similarly, there is recognition and respect for diversity and inclusion or there is not. Secondly, the principles of equity and inclusion apply to all dimensions of a person's life. Hence the need for intervention strategies that address every aspect of equity and inclusion.

The starting point for any discussion of the values informing school leadership has to be a recognition of the dignity and value of every human being *in their own right*. There cannot be 'degrees' of humanity. There can be no caveats or conditions that might be used to qualify the identity and integrity of a person. The essential value of every child has to be understood in terms of being human, without any artificial constructs or bureaucratic categorisations. Human dignity is not defined by states of consciousness, relative wealth or perceived social status. Likewise, the full range of educational outcomes has to be seen as having equal merit and status.

There are no comparative criteria that can be used scientifically, legitimately or morally to classify human beings on the basis of negative discriminatory treatment. Thus, gender, ethnicity, disability, relative measures of intelligence, varying degrees of athleticism, different artistic abilities, linguistic usages and social and cultural norms have to be regarded as descriptions of difference, and not as the basis for discrimination, whether personal or institutional. This point is fundamental to any discussion about respecting diversity and working to secure inclusion. Difference is the norm, and acknowledging diversity is the basis for strategies to safeguard inclusion based on equality and equity. This is a very powerful opportunity for pupil voice to be given its full expression and to explore its potential for informing the development of the school as a moral community that respects diversity and inclusion. It can be a salutary experience to push a wheelchair around a school that claims to be inclusive.

It would be wrong to take this approach for granted; it is very much a product of culture, the prevailing moral hegemony and conscious and deliberate choices. The moral consensus in Finland, for example, serves as the basis for a wide range of social, educational and 'taken-for-granted' policy assumptions. This cannot be replicated in other countries – it is a product of history, culture and national identity. However, consensus can be found in medical research project teams, sports teams, military units and local campaign groups. For values to be truly embedded in an education system, a number of fundamental choices have to be made, not the least of which is, what is to be the overarching core purpose of the education system?

Every education system has a dominant purpose. The Scandinavian countries tend to focus on well-being and social justice, and achievement follows. The English system is currently focused on performance to the effective exclusion of much of what is usually regarded as a holistic approach to education. Of course, most systems are a blend of these elements, but one is likely to dominate and this will give schooling its distinctive nature. Equally, schools will tend to identify with particular outcomes according to their social context, the nature of their intake and all the other variables that inform the identity of any organisation.

Developing morally confident leadership

It is probably fair to say that one of the most significant consequences of recent educational reforms in England, coupled with very high stakes accountability, is the increasing number of complex decisions that have to be taken at a school level by school leaders and governors. Many school leaders now have responsibility for decisions that were once taken by central and local government. The same is true of academy trusts. Therefore, leaders are accountable for choices that were once taken by people and committees which did not have to live with the consequences of those decisions on a daily basis. There is no hiding place – the buck stops at the head's desk.

These factors mean that the moral dimension of leadership could be seen as having the following elements:

- The confidence to challenge, question and 'speak truth to power'.
- Demonstrating the importance of consistency.
- The ability to recognise and respect alternative perspectives.
- Strategies to secure consent and consensus.
- The ability to translate principle into practice.

This list does not, of course, reflect the complexity and range of choices facing school leaders, and it would be wrong to attempt to simplify this complexity by introducing reductionist or formulaic responses.

> We understand better that in conditions of extremity, there are rarely to be found comfortingly simple categories of good and evil, guilt and innocent. We know more about the choices and compromises faced by men and women in hard times, and we are no longer quick to judge those who accommodate themselves to impossible situations. (Judt 2002: xiv)

While Judt is alluding to circumstances that would not normally be found in schools in England today, his basic observation is surely valid – there are more options, more conflicting alternatives and the implications of doing the wrong thing are greater than ever. A further compounding issue is that traditional roles and relationships have changed commensurately – historical patterns of hierarchy, control and sanctions have largely disappeared.

> The main characteristic of our new, lightweight moral tradition will be the principle of consent. Just as obedience to the commands of authority, whether God, state or any other centre of power, was the dominant characteristic of ancient traditions, so, today, is the consent of our reason and emotion. Today, we expect to be persuaded by coherent argument and the consequential results of particular policies. (Holloway 2004: 154)

Developing morally confident leadership has to be seen as a learning process, one of growth and development and engaging with the interaction of beliefs and practice. For Dewey, the pivotal component of this learning process is reflection, which is an:

> active, persistent and careful consideration of any belief or supposed form of knowledge in the light of the grounds that support it and further conclusions to which it leads … it includes a conscious and voluntary effort to establish belief upon a firm basis of evidence and rationality. (Dewey 1933: 23)

All of this implies leaders who are very clear and have high confidence about what they believe in and who see as their role as the translation of principle into practice. If equity and inclusion are to be embedded into a school's culture and working practices in a consistent and sustainable way, then leadership has to focus on the creation of a moral consensus. This, in turn, implies that leaders have a deep and authentic commitment to diversity and inclusion as moral principles. This has to be more than a policy to be implemented; it is fundamental to the integrity of leadership:

> authentic educational leadership must promote and support the core values of schooling. Authentic educational leaders challenge others to participate in the visionary activity of identifying in curriculum, in teaching and in learning what is worthwhile, what is worth doing and preferred ways of doing and acting together. (Duignan 2006: 128)

In practical terms, this means that we need to see the ethical dimension of leadership in terms of a number of behaviours and strategies.

The first element is developing a culture that aspires to objectivity and rationality and which sees morality as an expression of careful and thoughtful analysis based on evidence, respectful consideration of alternative perspectives and systematic approaches to problem solving. For Law (2006: 35) this means the ability to think critically, analytically and objectively combined with social understanding and self-awareness. What is challenging about Law's perspective is that it is his view as to what *children* ought to be able to do. This obviously implies that teachers and other adults in schools can use the same techniques with confidence, and that, in turn, clearly requires leaders who are confident in the application and advocacy of this approach based on thinking skills and higher order cognitive strategies. It is ironic that many of the techniques that Law advocates are found in primary schools that use Philosophy for

Children,* but these same techniques are often not sustained in secondary schools and are not always available to teachers, school leaders and governors. Similarly, many schools make use of Edward de Bono's 'six thinking hats' strategy. Sadly, it is not always used consistently across the school, and where it is used in classrooms it is not always used in staffrooms or school offices.

> How confident are you that your school is a moral community in which important decisions are made using the skills and strategies set out by Law?
>
> Is there a case for arguing that all members of the school community (from 5 (and younger) to 50 (and older)) should develop the skills and strategies outlined by Law?

The second element is the centrality of dialogue and engagement. Leaders develop a shared language and vocabulary so there is consistent usage of key concepts and a shared understanding of the underpinning values. Leaders tell stories of the preferred future of the school and develop scenarios to help all staff understand their contribution to the creation of the school as a moral community focused on securing equity and inclusion. Time is spent in team and staff meetings exploring the values of the school in practice, and securing informed consent to the principles and shared understanding of those principles in practice.

The third focus is on leaders as models. Leaders lead by example and are highly visible in demonstrating the practical implications of the school's core values. In practical terms this means that leaders are in the corridors, in the classroom, greeting pupils as they arrive in school and bidding them goodbye as they leave. As Law puts it:

> We need personal experience of what living virtuously is like before we are in a position to appreciate that this really is how we ought to behave. And we are only able to have that experience if we have been trained, disciplined and habituated into acting well. (Law 2006: 125)

For many leaders, these strategies reflect the central component of their working lives. There is little doubt that a sense of moral purpose and

---

* See http://www.p4c.com.

vocation is a pivotal factor in the approach of the vast majority of school leaders to their professional work. What this chapter has argued for is a more explicit focus on equity and inclusion.

The final point to be made about moral confidence is that sometimes it may require a public challenge or commitment – to assert that the emperor is not wearing any clothes and to question dogma, bad evidence and abuse of power:

> educators need to become provocateurs; they need to take a stand while refusing to be involved in either a cynical relativism or doctrinaire politics. In part, I mean that central to intellectual life is the pedagogical and political imperative that academics engage in rigorous social criticism while becoming a stubborn force for challenging false prophets, deconstructing social relations that promote material and symbolic violence, and speaking the 'truth' to dominant forms of power and authority. (Giroux 1997: 268)

As with all professional learning, it seems that finding the opportunity to engage in rich dialogue with colleagues, to review and reflect, and to question and challenge prevailing orthodoxies is fundamental to building confidence and informing action. The development of moral confidence – clarity about what the 'right things' are – is the product of linking theory and practice, analysing that practice, reviewing and reflecting, and then consolidating and embedding authentic and consistent strategies. It is clear that, for most educational systems, the moral choices will grow in complexity and so school leaders will need to grow in moral confidence and develop the ability to translate principle into practice.

Leadership as a moral activity

Classify each of the following components of your leadership of change as A, B, C or D, according to the extent to which it shows:

A. High confidence and is well established in principle and practice.

B. Emergent practice for some of the time.

C. Some awareness but no consistent practice.

D. No awareness.

Leadership behaviours	**Rating/ evidence**	**Implications/ action**
Confident understanding of the fundamental principles underpinning education in Britain		
A strong sense of personal values leading to moral confidence in a range of situations		
Seeing leadership as moral action based in evidence – a willingness to challenge, question and hold to account		
Confidence in securing consensus and consent and developing the school as a moral community		
The courage to speak the truth to power		
Confidence in modelling professional behaviour and engaging in dialogue to develop understanding and commitment in others		
A passionate commitment to equity and inclusion		

Chapter 4

Learning as the core purpose of school leadership

Is there anything totally new to be said about teaching and learning? Probably not. Is there a need to constantly refresh and renew our thinking about teaching and learning? Absolutely. This chapter tests the hypothesis that the core purpose of leadership in education is learning by reviewing the following issues:

- Is it clear in your school that the core purpose of leadership is to secure effective learning for all?
- How explicit is the link between effective teaching and learning and closing the gap?
- How secure is the consensus around the principles of effective learning?
- To what extent are teaching and learning evidence and data based?
- Is the school a genuine learning community in which every member of the community, irrespective of age or status, is able to learn?

The relationship between teaching, learning and the curriculum is a complex one, with each element varying in its degree of perceived significance over time and in different contexts. What is clear is that the debate about the nature of the curriculum, and its relationship with teaching, is clearer and more confident than the debate about the nature and place of learning.

There seems to be a tacit assumption that if I teach the curriculum in an appropriate way then you will learn. Indeed, much of the rhetoric around the curriculum is essentially posited on a delivery model – the job of the teacher is to deliver content (information) pertinent to the subject being taught. Until quite recently, lesson planning was often seen in terms of teacher activity rather than pupil learning. Ofsted's move away from classifying lessons to identifying progress is symptomatic of a movement away from assessing the delivery of curriculum content towards identifying successful pupil learning.

There seems little doubt that there has been a significant shift towards a focus on learning in schools – senior staff have more explicit responsibility for the quality of learning than ever before and there is a demonstrable shift in emphasis in the work of middle leaders from managing resources to enabling learning. However, modern schools are very complex organisations. The range of demands on school leaders seems to grow ever more demanding and there are numerous technical aspects of the role that might detract from learning. The significance and status of learning in a school might be judged against the following criteria:

- The priorities identified in job descriptions.
- The existence of senior roles focused on securing effective learning and progress for all pupils.
- The extent to which internal accountability focuses on learning.
- The amount of time that the head teacher and senior staff spend in classrooms – monitoring, modelling and coaching.
- The focus on the quality of learning in team, leadership and staff meetings.
- The emphasis on learning in CPD programmes and appraisal and performance management.
- Governors and trustees who are confident in holding school leaders to account for the quality of learning.

Does your school have a common language of learning with a shared vocabulary and consistent practice across all adults and pupils?

How central is learning to leadership in your school?

Modes of learning

An alternative perspective might be to move away from what has been delivered, or how much progress has been made, to what has been understood and therefore informs the ability to act. Dewey catches this crucial relationship:

> We state emphatically that, *upon its intellectual side education consists in the formation of wide-awake, careful, thorough habits of thinking.* Of course intellectual learning includes the amassing and retention of information. But information is an undigested burden unless it is understood. It is *knowledge* only as its material is *comprehended.* (1933: 78; our emphasis)

Building on this perspective, learning needs to be seen as the vehicle for converting information into knowledge and so enabling and empowering learners. It might be helpful to draw a distinction between Dewey's model of learning as creating knowledge – what might be described as deep learning, and its converse – shallow learning that tends to be focused on the memorisation and replication of information. There is also the need to recognise the importance of profound learning – that dimension of personal development which is usually expressed through insight and wisdom.

Shallow learning requires the uncritical acceptance of facts, rote learning and seeing various elements of information as unrelated and isolated themes. In a shallow learning situation, learners are passive, the emphasis is on coverage of content, assessment is summative and content is often quickly forgotten (e.g.'summer loss'). The teacher controls the learning by keeping the learner compliant and dependent. Shallow learning is effectively transmissive and is easily assessable in terms of right and wrong answers. Shallow learning is important and significant if it is regarded, not as an end in itself, but rather as a stage in developing language skills and laying the foundations of information that may enable deep learning to take place. Practice is an important example of this – the greatest musicians, athletes and dancers practise every day in order to have the confidence to perform at the highest level.

Deep learning, by contrast, is focused on the creation of knowledge through the development of understanding. It involves the analysis and synthesis of facts to generate conceptual models and frameworks, integrating prior learning and cross-referencing to other themes and subjects. Deep leaning is active and has depth and breadth. Assessment of deep learning has to be formative and negotiated. The content of the curriculum is remembered *and* codified. Deep learning is controlled by the learner who understands the learning process, with the teacher as facilitator, mentor and co-constructor of knowledge.

Profound learning is about the creation of wisdom where understanding deepens into intuitive thinking and behaviour. Profound learning is being able to interpret the music to allow improvisation with confidence. Profound learning is confidence in thinking in an abstract way in a second language. Profound learning is not a function of age or academic attainment but rather higher order thinking and understanding and the ability to express ideas and emotions in very different ways. Profound learning is manifested in the work of the sculptor and the brick-layer, the composer and the musician, the poet and the child reading and comprehending language. As Perkins (1995: 206) observes: 'students need more than traditional academic skills. They need practical coping skills around reading, writing, solving problems, capitalizing on their strengths to overcome weaknesses, and so on.'

> Does your own experience as a teacher confirm or challenge the idea of shallow, deep and profound modes of learning?
>
> To what extent is there a consensus in your school that there needs to be a balance of teaching strategies to make shallow learning as efficient as possible, to ensure that deep learning is a consistent experience and that there are opportunities for profound learning as part of the entitlement of all?

The what and how of learning

There is a long-standing, and often rather recondite, debate on the balance in the curriculum between the information to be presented (in the form of subject knowledge) and the means by which that information becomes knowledge (the movement from shallow to deep learning). The somewhat arbitrary dichotomy between content and process has led to a sometimes extreme polarisation when, in fact, as is so often the case, the truth lies somewhere in the middle. What is needed is a balance between subject knowledge and the skills and strategies necessary to make sense of that knowledge. The truth lies between a Gradgrindian approach to facts and a Rousseauian model founded on a naive belief in a sensory-based education. Children need to know facts, but they also need to know how to make sense of their place in nature and society.

To take an obvious example, studying history involves having access to a range of information that is appropriate to the particular theme or topic being studied. However, learning a particular chronology is no substitute for understanding the problems of causality in making sense of social trends. Likewise, mastery of the periodic table is no guarantee of an appreciation of the scientific method, and memorising a poem is a necessary but not sufficient basis for engaging with a literary text.

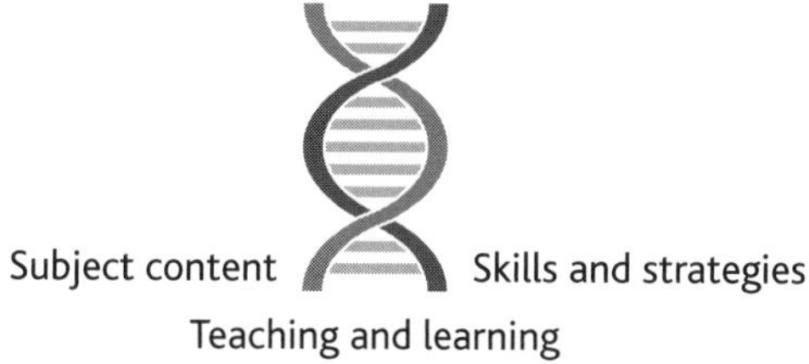

Figure 4.1. The learning helix

Figure 4.1 uses the interconnected strands of the helix as a model for the effective curriculum, with one strand being defined as subject content, the other strand as the skills and strategies necessary to engage with the content, and the connections linking the strands as the teaching and learning strategies that enable the interaction of the 'what' and the 'how'. Each element of the model is equally valid and significant. However, the 'how' strand is what many employers say they are looking for in terms of employability and potential to succeed in employment:

> We know that enjoying a school performance gives an opportunity to learn about the subject disciplines of dance, drama, art, music, English and probably design and technology, but it extends to many of the skills that employers say are vital in the working world today. (Waters 2013: 268)

Employability and success in higher education require both a broad range of knowledge and, crucially, the skills and strategies to apply that knowledge. Only schools and universities are really concerned with 'subjects'; most engineering work involves some knowledge of, say, physics but at least as important is the ability to build a bridge on time and under budget. This involves a range of problem-solving skills and human qualities such as personal resilience, emotional literacy and personal integrity.

> What is the ratio of time spent on subject content and learner skills and strategies in your school?
>
> To what extent are you developing confident self-managing learners who are meta-cognitive?

Of course, learners need to know the factual basis of the subjects they are studying, but the ability to engage with that information is just as significant. There is no point in studying a language and passing an examination but not being able to actually use it. Likewise, the purpose of studying a science or history is not just to replicate appropriate information, but rather to create knowledge by explaining, analysing, justifying, comparing and synthesising. There always has been a tendency in education to reduce the world into teachable units. In 1895, two Belgians, Paul Otlet and Henri La Fontaine, created the Universal Bibliographic Repertory – a collection of 15 million index cards that sought to collect and organise all information. It came to be called the Mundaneum and prefigured the Internet in many ways. However, learning to access 15 million index cards is not the same as creating knowledge through developing understanding.

The situation where the ability to replicate information accurately is more valued than the ability to make sense of that information is the starting point for our discussion in this chapter. We need to see subject content, information and intellectual skills as being in a symbiotic relationship, combining to create knowledge that is evidenced and assessed in demonstrated understanding.

If we look at how teaching and learning are organised in schools, then in the primary school the approach is chronological and assumes that each cohort is homogeneous and all children progress at the same rate through the school. In the secondary school, it is the subject that provides the organisational rationale. In both cases, a helpful way of understanding what determines the nature of teaching and learning is the underpinning principle that form follows function. The organisational structure of schools (their form) provides a very clear indicator as to their core purpose (or function). While the public aspiration may be the learning of the individual, this is belied by the reality of the actual experience of school. Thus, if a school is organised on a chronological basis, with compartmentalisation based on subjects, and if teachers are deployed on those same principles, then the chances are it is a secondary school.

Only in the special school and in early years provision (and in the Waldorf (Steiner) and Montessori philosophies) is the child the starting point for designing the learning process in response to the needs of the individual. In essence, the historical model of schooling is teacher centric in the same way that many organisations are leader centric. If the accepted role of the teacher or leader is questioned and the perspective shifts to the learner or follower, then some fundamental assumptions come under scrutiny. In particular, the issue of control becomes central – who decides?

It is very interesting to see what happens when certain key criteria are changed – for example, the move from police force to police service, from War Office to Ministry of Defence, from middle manager to middle leaders, from senior management team to school leadership team, from teacher to facilitator and from curriculum as delivered content to curriculum as the vehicle for learning.

This chapter will now explore what happens when learning becomes the basis for the structure and organisation of the school. The problem is that there isn't the same level of confidence about talking about learning as there is about the subject content of the curriculum or about teaching itself. In some schools, there is no shared vocabulary about learning that enables adults, pupils and their parents to engage in meaningful conversations about learning; instead, the conversations are about successful engagement with the curriculum in terms of acquisition rather than understanding.

> How far, and in what ways, is the learning experience of pupils in your school personal to the individual?

Developing a shared model of learning

What follows are seven propositions designed to serve as starting points for a debate about the nature of the learning-centred school – in particular, the school that seeks to move towards equity by ensuring access to deep learning for every member of the school community. We are not offering these propositions as definitive or exhaustive, rather they are designed to support and encourage dialogue so that education professionals can take control of the teaching and learning process.

1. Every learner is unique

Although there are many generic factors influencing learning, the range is so diverse and the possible permutations so great that it becomes essential to start with the individual learner. One way of passing time in the supermarket is to covertly assess the contents of other people's trolleys. It quickly becomes clear that although there are many items in common, each trolley reflects the unique lifestyle choices of that household in terms of both quality and quantity. It might be far simpler for supermarkets to offer generic trolleys (based, for example, on class prejudices or eating for well-being) that have been costed in advance. But the whole point of doing our own shopping is that we are different and we reflect that difference in our most basic needs.

If a genuine attempt is to be made in the education system to respect and respond to the uniqueness of each learner, then the learning profile and personal dispositions and choices of each individual has to be the starting point for any learning strategy. For Gardner (1999: 245), 'Possessing different kinds of minds [means that] individuals represent information and knowledge in idiosyncratic ways.'

There is now increasing confidence that we can make even stronger assertions about the centrality and distinctiveness of the individual learner:

> Our evidence makes it crystal clear that treating children as blank slates or empty vessels, using a factory model of schooling, and arbitrarily imposing the same targets for everyone are approaches that work against, rather than with natural child development. Our schools and our educational policies will be improved if they are designed to respond to naturally occurring individual differences in ability and development. (Asbury and Plomin 2014: 12)

The ongoing findings of the Human Genome Project mean that we are becoming increasingly aware of the complex interactions of our genetic inheritance and environmental factors. In education, we are feeling far less secure, possibly because the implications are potentially so challenging to prevailing orthodoxies. Every teacher recognises the interaction of nature and nurture, but perhaps we need to focus as much on the nature as we do on the nurture.

The aims or mission statements of many schools might be seen as a series of public promises. Usually these promises are made in terms of the individual, yet the experience in many schools is largely generic. For most pupils the system works well, but it might be that it is the most vulnerable pupils who are most in need of a personalised approach.

Another crucial element in respecting the dignity and uniqueness of every learner is the extent to which they are able to choose – that is, to be active participants in the key decisions informing their education. In many ways, choice is one of the defining characteristics of life in the 21st century. There are more options available than ever before – from the banal (a local supermarket offers 32 different types of olive oil – why?) to the profound (choices about faith and personal relationships).

The practical implications of focusing on the learner as a unique individual point to the personalisation of learning. This, in turn, involves:

- The profiling of the learner in terms of motivation, engagement, skills (e.g. literacy and numeracy), social context, learning dispositions and necessary resources.
- The development of a personal learning plan that is negotiated and reviewed and serves as the basis for the learner becoming self-managing.
- The provision of a wide portfolio of learning opportunities involving multimedia provision of a range of themes and topics.
- Negotiated assessment with an emphasis on formative assessment and moving towards summative assessment based on the model used by the Associated Board of the Royal Schools of Music (i.e. levels 1–8 with learners able to take the appropriate level at any age).
- The development of appropriate levels of choice over what is learnt, when it is learnt, how it is learnt and who it is learnt with.
- The movement towards a school structure based on stage not age.

It may be that one of the major leadership challenges, in terms of learning, is to find ways of reconciling personal choice with organisational effectiveness. It is almost certainly the case that personalising learning can make a significant contribution towards closing the gap and securing the entitlement of every learner to an appropriate education.

> What does your school's aims statement say about the individual learner? To what extent are your aspirations translated into the consistent experience of every pupil? For example, is choice a function of age and ability or an entitlement for all?
>
> How much choice is available to the adults in school?
>
> How much guidance is available to the pupils about making personal choices, from diet and lifestyle to learning and development?

2. Learning is a social process

Although a great deal can be learnt by an individual working on their own, there is abundant evidence that learning is an essentially social process – the long history of teachers, tutors, facilitators, mentors and coaches bears abundant witness to the importance of relationships in learning. Likewise, the importance of parent, grandparent and peer support is a demonstrably significant component of successful learning. There is clear evidence from comparative anatomical studies that in the higher apes brain size is directly correlated with the quality of social interaction (Dunbar 2010). Learning requires interaction; however, it is not enough just to have a teacher or equivalent. The learning relationship needs to be a positive one in terms of the quality and integrity of all learning situations. It is also important to stress that the quality of relationships is not just a matter of teacher–learner; it is equally importantly to do with learner–learner relationships. Day and his colleagues (2009: 244) capture the essence of the link between relationships and learning when they observe:

> Some recent studies show that trust remains a powerful and strong predictor of student achievement even after the effects of student background, prior achievement, race, and gender have been taken into account. Therefore, school leaders need to pay careful attention to the trust they engender in teachers, students, and parents if they wish to improve organizational performance still further.

Trust is a prerequisite for any collaborative human activity – from the most intimate relationships and the deepest friendships to professional relationships, working in teams and living in a community, trust is the essential ingredient.

For learning to take place there seems to be a need for challenge as well as trust. Empathy is a critical element, as are sensitivity, responsiveness and respect as conveyed through the core skills of listening and attending. These aspects are expressed in two particular areas: firstly, the relationship between teacher and learner and, secondly, the emotional climate of the school. The relationship between teacher and learner is best understood with reference to Vygotsky's concept of the zone of proximal development which describes the gap between what the learner working alone can achieve and what can be achieved with the support of a skilled helper, facilitator, mentor or teacher (see Sternberg 1990: 242).

The quality and integrity of the learning relationship has enormous potential to optimise the learner's potential and to significantly enhance their progress.

The emotional climate of the school might be best understood in terms of the emotional literacy of the school as a community – that is, the behaviours, strategies and norms that inform relationships as well as the policies and resources that are devoted to optimising positive relationships. There are numerous formulations of the possible components of a model of emotional literacy, but a generic framework might include the following elements:

- Recognising emotions in oneself and others and developing strategies to manage those emotions.
- Being aware of personal strengths and areas for development.
- Being empathic and sensitive to others, articulating concern.
- Being sensitive to differences and respecting and valuing alternative perspectives.
- Listening and responding appropriately (e.g. 'Yes and …' not 'Yes but …').
- Analysing problems and developing effective responses.
- Engaging with others and building positive relationships.
- Summarising and synthesising, building consensus.
- Cooperating, negotiating, and managing conflict using team-based approaches.
- Help seeking and help giving.
- Monitoring and reviewing tasks and processes.

These skills and behaviours are relevant and should be available to all members of the school community from 5 (and younger) to 50 (and older). We would argue that they are central to effective learning, managing, leading and being together in a community. In essence, the skills for learning are the skills for living and working, and they need to be embedded in every dimension of the school's life:

> Emotional literacy involves factors such as people understanding their own and others' emotional states; learning to manage their emotions and empathise with others. It also includes the recognition that emotional literacy is both an individual development and a collective activity and is both about self-development and the building of community so that one's own sense of emotional well-being grows along with that of others. (Matthews 2012: 253)

If one of the functions of schools is to prepare young people for a life in relationships, living in a community and for employment, then it must be recognised that life involves collaborative working and learning. Success in relationships and as a member of any type of community requires emotional literacy. The majority of jobs involve collaborative problem solving, and most workers, right across the employment spectrum, cooperate to complete tasks, meet deadlines and find effective solutions to a diverse range of issues. Likewise, learning involves multiple alternative social relationships; in schools, these need to include relationships with other learners. The school's structures and relationships need to optimise the opportunities for problem-based collaborative working if it is to genuinely prepare people for lives other than teaching. In practical terms this means:

- Recognising that personal relationships are primarily a moral issue at the heart of the school's values and purpose.
- Working towards building a high trust culture as the essential precursor to improvement and learning.
- Focusing leadership in the school on developing an emotionally literate community, largely through modelling and dialogue.
- Providing training to ensure consistent usage of the interpersonal skills necessary to secure effective learning, notably listening and empathy.
- Deeply embedding a culture of review and reflection (i.e. 'What went well?') that permeates learning activities, meetings and all social interactions.

How emotionally literate are your colleagues?

What proportion of the issues that you are confronted with can be attributed to a lack of emotional literacy?

What are you doing to build the school as an emotionally literate community?

3. Learning can take place anytime, anywhere and with anyone

Most young people in Britain are in school for about 16 per cent of each year; hopefully they are getting enough sleep, which should amount to about 40 per cent of the year, which means they are actively involved in living and learning outside school for 44 per cent of each year. Thus 'going to school to learn' is a fundamental misconception. Children should be going to school for certain types of learning; they are always learning, even in their dreams.

What this points to is a holistic view of the curriculum as the combined experience of all the possibilities that enhance the learning of children and young people. Of course, what might be called the formal curriculum – academic subjects that are assessed in some way – does have a particular status and significance. But, in most maintained schools, it might be that we need to question the notion that only 16 per cent of the year is available and look to different sorts of provision and resourcing to secure the full potential of a range of learning experiences:

> A really important aspect of the organisation of learning is the extent to which different dimensions of real life in the twenty-first century can be incorporated within curriculum planning ... They deal with things such as enterprise and entrepreneurship. They focus on cultural diversity, identity and belonging. They encourage young people to be active citizens. (Waters 2013: 275)

There are no situations when a human being is not engaged in some type of learning. Concerns are increasingly expressed about children not being 'school ready' but a greater concern is surely that they should be 'life ready', and this involves being effective learners in every context of their lives. It is a well-established principle that the most significant learning, in a range of key respects, is the learning that takes place in the child's family, community and peer group. In some cases, the only recognition of learning beyond the school is homework. This is a missed opportunity to roll out strategies that recognise parents as first educators. We should also acknowledge that literacy, oracy and social interactions are the basis for all learning and that these are significantly informed by contextual factors like parenting, community values and social class.

The implications of this perspective might be summarised as follows:

- The need to engage parents as active partners in their children's education, particularly with respect to language and social development, through play and rich language opportunities.
- The importance of seeing the community as a learning resource through greater mutual interaction with local agencies, organisations and individuals (e.g. through volunteering and working for community service projects).
- Joining one of the many youth organisations that focus on a wide range of social and learning-based activities (e.g. the Red Cross, Scouts and Guides, the Duke of Edinburgh's Award).
- Moving away from the notion of after-school clubs into a range of clubs that provide activities that are complementary to school-based learning (e.g. chess, astronomy, learning to cycle and drive, subjects that might be marginalised by the English Baccalaureate).
- Presenting music and drama activities as integral to the curriculum and important opportunities for personal development.
- Developing international links through the use of social media.
- Making groups of pupils responsible for different aspects of the school site (e.g. gardens, allotments, wildlife conservation areas).
- Building links with professional and amateur sports clubs.
- Entrepreneurial activities which develop both a sense of service and financial understanding.
- Citizenship and active leadership in the school and the community.

Does your school's learning strategy acknowledge that your pupils spend almost five times as much time away from school as in it?

What strategies are in use to enrich the curriculum so that it is not constrained by external testing?

How rich is the engagement with your local community as a source of alternative modes of learning?

4. Intelligence can be learnt

Intelligence is generally understood as an expression of cognitive capacity and ability. It is fundamentally informed by genetic inheritance and neurological functioning, but as with many aspects of genetic and brain functioning, intelligence is open to mediation and development. There are many ways of classifying intelligence. IQ remains the dominant model (although there are anxieties about its reliability, validity and cultural determinism), while Gardner's model of multiple intelligences remains a powerful, if contentious, alternative perspective.

Intelligence is generally described in terms of the cognitive abilities involved in creating knowledge, thinking conceptually and working with abstract ideas, understanding logic and the processes involved in reasoning, recognising and explaining relationships, exercising choice and, crucially, articulating and justifying not just what is understood but also how it is understood. The development of these characteristics clearly relate to levels of progression within the education system, although it would be wrong to make a direct correlation between cognitive development and chronology. What is clear is that intelligence can be developed and enhanced by education. In their meta-analysis of the key cognitive factors influencing successful learning, Schneider and Stern (2010) identify the 10 variables that, in various permutations, seem to determine the development of understanding. They suggest that good learning environments should:

- Stimulate learners to be mentally active.
- Address prior knowledge.

- Integrate fragmented pieces of knowledge into meaningful structures.
- Balance concepts, skills and meta-cognitive competence.
- Help learners to organise knowledge hierarchically.
- Provide models and frameworks to help learners organise their knowledge (e.g. lesson structures, modelling, displays).
- Recognise that successful learning may be inhibited by the limited capacity of working memory.
- Recognise that learning is the product of the complex interplay of cognition, motivation and emotion.
- Enable learners to transfer knowledge between contexts.
- 'Recognise that time and effort invested in practising problem-solving and extending one's knowledge base are among the most important factors influencing the success of learning' (2010: 84).

Adey (2012: 211) shows that there are programmes which have successfully demonstrated that better thinking can be positively affected by appropriate teaching strategies – perhaps the most convincing evidence of the plasticity of intelligence:

> A recent evaluation of the Philosophy for Children (P4C) programme in one local authority's schools showed an effective size on cognitive abilities of 0.48 ... the gains made by the experimental group over the controls was maintained for at least two years. ...
>
> The cognitive acceleration (CA) approach has been demonstrating big effects for years ... students who used CA in science ... scored about 1 grade higher in their GCSE science, mathematics and English compared with matched controls.

Adey's work shows that carefully designed interventions can have a significant impact on a learner's cognitive capacity and thereby on their academic performance. Crucially, he demonstrates that intelligence is not fixed and therefore appropriate interventions will raise achievement. His work is reinforced by the Sutton Trust–Education Endowment Foundation investigation into teaching and learning strategies which make a significant difference to pupil attainment. The Sutton Trust–Education Endowment Foundation Toolkit identifies meta-cognition and self-regulation strategies as being some of the most potent and effective, generating high levels of impact for very low cost:

> Meta-cognition and self-regulation approaches have consistently high levels of impact, with pupils making an average of eight months' additional progress. The evidence indicates that teaching these strategies can be particularly effective for low achieving and older pupils.
>
> These strategies are usually more effective when taught in collaborative groups so learners can support each other and make their thinking explicit through discussion. The potential impact of these approaches is very high, but can be difficult to achieve as they require pupils to take greater responsibility for their learning and develop their understanding of what is required to succeed.*

The practical implications of developing strategies to support thinking across the school might include:

- Providing training in meta-cognitive strategies for all pupils and all staff – becoming a thinking school.
- School leaders modelling cognitive strategies in all aspects of the school's working (e.g. using restorative justice strategies rather than punishment-based approaches**).
- Embedding cognitive strategies across the curriculum, ensuring consistent application and assuming their use in all activities.
- Developing a culture based on objective evidence, rational dialogue and reasoned interactions – a culture of explanation, reasoning and justification.
- Focusing pupil voice on developing and enhancing learning and teaching.

---

* See https://educationendowmentfoundation.org.uk/toolkit/toolkit-a-z/meta-cognitive-and-self-regulation-strategies/.

** See, for example, the work of Restorative Justice 4 Schools at http://www.restorativejustice4schools.co.uk.

> What strategies are in use in your school that demonstrate the shared belief of the staff in the plasticity of intelligence?
>
> How much status and significance is given to cognitive interventions, especially for disadvantaged students, as per the advice contained in the Sutton Trust–Education Endowment Foundation Toolkit?
>
> Is your school a thinking school?

5. Learning is a neurological function

Learning takes place in the brain – essentially, it is an electrochemical process of infinite complexity. Successful learning is a sophisticated equation involving a range of variables with many complex interactions. Neurologists and cognitive scientists are extremely wary about some of the claims and practices emerging from their research. Although neurological science and cognitive psychology have made major progress in enhancing our understanding of brain functioning, it is not yet possible to build robust bridges between research and practice. We have learnt to be appropriately cautious about the claims made for Brain Gym, learning styles and Omega 3.

Nevertheless, there is much that can be applied, however indirectly, from the work of cognitive neuroscientists, notably Professor Sarah-Jayne Blakemore of University College London. Her work has focused on the neuroscience of adolescence – namely, why teenagers are the way they are. It has long been understood and accepted that the first three years of life are essential in terms of personal potential because this is a period of high neuroplasticity. (Although this fact is yet to be fully recognised in policy or practice – for example, shouldn't the early years have a disproportionately large share of the education budget?) What Blakemore and her colleagues have demonstrated is that early adolescence is a period of equal significance in terms of neural development and a number of behavioural characteristics that may be highly significant in understanding the optimum conditions for adolescent learning.

The major elements seem to be:

- Heightened self-awareness.
- A propensity for risk taking.
- A strong sense of the social self, especially peer influences.
- An emerging sense of personal beliefs.

Equally significant is the fact that a key element in mature behaviour, the ability to plan, is not fully developed in early adolescence, and the fact that the body clock of teenagers is totally different to that of any other stage of human development. This is due to synaptic pruning – the brain sorting out what is and is not important. According to Professor Blakemore, there are many practical implications from the developments in cognitive neuroscience for how we organise learning in schools:

> One of the contributions to education that neuroscience is capable of making is illuminating the nature of learning itself. It is unlikely that there is one single all-purpose type of learning for everything. In terms of brain structures involved learning mathematics differs from learning to read, which differs from learning to play the piano. Each memory system relies on a different brain system and develops at a slightly different time. (Blakemore and Frith 2005: 139)

There are numerous areas of neuroscience that open up the possibility of interventions that might enhance the potential of learners to learn more effectively and so maximise their potential to succeed. Three areas that seem to be free of the contamination of pseudo-science are the potential to enhance memory, the place of challenge in human cognitive activity and the importance of practice.

Memory is a vital element of learning and serves as the foundation for developing understanding. Perhaps the simplest way of demonstrating the centrality of memory to learning is that without it we would simply work through simple reflexes and stereotyped behaviours. In many respects, learning is memorisation in the sense of securing changes in behaviour, skill and knowledge and being able to call on them at will. If you cannot remember, you cannot demonstrate that you have learnt. Given this basic fact, it is perplexing that so little attention is paid to memory in most schools. Memory can be enhanced through practice and the use of some very simple strategies. Correspondingly, the effectiveness of an individual's memory can be diagnosed. On this basis, it is possible to argue that specific interventions designed to enhance memory should be part of the daily routines in every classroom. Key elements in developing memory are challenge and practice.

Challenge is significant because of its apparent potential to secure interest and engagement. A central proposition of this discussion is that challenge is the basis of all effective learning, and that human beings are at their most effective as learners when faced with a challenge, a problem to solve or an enquiry to follow. One way of understanding human evolution is to see it in terms of an increasing capacity to solve problems collaboratively. Challenge-based approaches are how we move from shallow learning based on the replication of information to deep learning based on the creation of knowledge, personal understanding and the ability to act and apply.

Practice seems to be a fundamental component of success across a wide range of human activities. Most educationalists share legitimate concerns about the potentially negative implications of rote learning – it is properly perceived as both instrumental and reductionist. However, if you were to say to a concert pianist, professional dancer or world-class athlete that they were wasting their time practising, they would give you short shrift. Effective structured practice, with support and feedback, is just about the only way of achieving sustained improvement. Performance is directly related to working hard and practising.

Practice, of itself, could be literally pointless. Practice with the support of a coach, using effective feedback and set against clearly defined outcomes has the potential to be transformative. Underpinning every aspect of the neurological perspectives on education is the idea that there is no real substitute for persistence, determination and the willingness to work hard. This is not so much about 'practice makes perfect' as 'practice makes permanent'. We learn to ride a bicycle safely and enjoyably through practice – every time we ride our bike we reinforce that transition from anxious wobbling to assured cycling because we are practising.

Here some are some practical applications of a neurologically based learning culture:

- Start the school day later – teenagers need sleep if they are to learn effectively.

- Start each day with 10–15 minutes of challenge-based 'warm-up' activities (e.g. anagrams, cryptic clues, memory tests, logic puzzles, Sudoku, concentration exercises) – individual and shared, personal and competitive.
- Build on learners' prior knowledge by getting them to identify issues and challenges (i.e. problematise the topic). Introduce topics in terms of challenges and problems rather than content.
- All students engage in sustained personal research projects (which may form the basis of homework) over a period of time.
- Once a year (or once a term) get the entire school involved in a 'challenge week' involving activities outside the standard curriculum.
- Introduce coaching to support practice and feedback. Develop peer coaching.
- Set up a 'challenge committee' to be responsible for developing challenges across the school and curriculum.
- Institute a 'challenge of the day' designed to get the entire school focused on an issue or problem (e.g. 'Find out why …' 'Tell me how …').
- Set up a chess club and other clubs to play games based on strategy, memory, practice and problem solving. Introduce debating.
- In addition to sports day and house sports competitions, organise a thinking Olympics.
- Introduce Philosophy for Children (www.p4c.com), the work of the Philosophy Foundation (www.philosophy-foundation.org) and Sapere (www.sapere.org.uk). Use assemblies to develop school community debates on moral issues and themes.

> How far is classroom practice in your school evidence based?
>
> How are school leaders kept up to date with the latest research on teaching and learning from the Sutton Trust–Education Endowment Foundation and the like?

6. Learning, progress and achievement require a growth mindset

Dweck (2006) contends that people can be placed on a continuum according to their implicit views about where ability comes from. Some believe their success is based on innate ability – these individuals are said to have a 'fixed' theory of intelligence (fixed mindset). Others, who believe their success is based on having the opposite mindset – which involves hard work, learning, training and doggedness – are said to have a 'growth' or an 'incremental' theory of intelligence (growth mindset). We know from the work of John Hattie, Carol Dweck and the University of Durham/Sutton Trust/Education Endowment Foundation report on the effective use of the pupil premium (Higgins et al. 2011) that feedback is one of the most powerful strategies to raise pupil achievement because it is a key means of supporting the development of a growth mindset.

For feedback to really make an impact on an individual's learning, potential achievement and possible success, the teacher/facilitator/coach has to focus on developing a growth mindset. This means that effective feedback should:

- Be specific, accurate and clear (e.g. 'It was good because you ...' rather than just 'correct').
- Compare what a learner is doing right now compared with what they have done wrong before (e.g. 'I can see you were focused on improving X as it is much better than last time').
- Encourage and support further effort (i.e. getting a balance between support and challenge).
- Be given sparingly so that it is meaningful – too much feedback can stop learners working out what they need to do for themselves.
- Be about what is right more often than about what is wrong (e.g. 'This section is excellent because ...' or 'I thought this was the best part because ...').

Feedback should be about complex or challenging tasks or goals because this is likely to emphasise the importance of effort and perseverance as well as be more valued by the pupils. The central message of Dweck's work is that there is no substitute for hard work and practice reinforced and supported by skilled feedback within a 'growth mindset environment' in which people can thrive. According to Dweck (2006: 141), this involves leaders creating school cultures that:

- See skills as learnable.
- Convey that the organisation values learning and perseverance, not just ready-made genius or talent.
- Give feedback in a way that promotes learning and future success.
- Present managers as resources for learning.

> In what ways is the principle of the growth mindset used in your school?
>
> In what ways is it applied to pupils?
>
> In what ways is it applied to staff?

7. Learning is assessed through understanding

In many ways, assessment is the most problematic dimension of learning. The characteristics of the assessment process have had a very significant impact on the nature of the teaching and learning experience. It can be safely argued that one of the most significant factors in teaching and learning from Years 6 to 11 is the impact of summative assessment coupled with high stakes accountability.

The purpose of assessment for learning is to provide feedback to the learner in order to support engagement with the learning process, demonstrate progress, secure understanding and indicate future directions in the learning journey. Assessment for learning is a vital source of evidence to inform the design of learning and teaching strategies. Judgements need to be as objective and transparent as possible and use agreed and authoritative criteria. To reiterate Dewey's point from the start of this chapter, learning creates '*knowledge* only as its material is *comprehended*' (1933: 78). In other words, we can only be confident that learning has taken place to the extent that the learner actually understands and can apply what has been learnt.

Feedback needs to be formative, aspirational, challenging and indicate ways forward for the learner. Assessment for learning must be integrated into learning to learn and meta-cognitive strategies and be understood by all involved in the learning process. Formative assessment should be derived from negotiations with the learner, which might include the topic to be assessed, the criteria for assessment, the nature of the assessment process, agreed outcomes and the link to summative assessment. Crucially, assessment should reflect both *what* is learnt and *how* it has been learnt – that is, an equal focus on content and process.

The essential criterion of assessment is the demonstration of understanding. This involves the successful use of a range of intellectual strategies and skills, including:

- Explanation: the ability to communicate and share meaning using alternative perspectives.
- Classification: the ability to analyse and codify using a range of criteria and models.
- Exemplification: the capacity to describe, demonstrate and illustrate.
- Research: confidence in seeking evidence and designing investigations to produce relevant data.
- Challenge: a tendency to ask 'why', 'how' and 'what if' questions – confidence in questioning, challenging and being challenged.
- Synthesis: the ability to contrast and identify common characteristics – the ability to integrate ideas from a range of sources and show relationships.
- Causality: the ability to recognise logical relationships and differences – the ability to see and make connections between cause and effect.
- Generalisation: the ability to formulate hypotheses and see patterns.
- Action: the ability and confidence to translate theory into practice (e.g. the ability to hold a confident conversation in a second language).

- Meta-cognition: self-awareness and self-direction – demonstrating reflexivity, 'knowing what and knowing how'.

The key issues with assessment are the consistent usage of appropriate terminology and embedding formative and summative feedback into the learning process – that is, using assessment as a vehicle for learning. At its best, assessment for understanding builds the confidence to perform well when summative assessment is required. If deep learning is to be embedded into the school's ways of thinking and working, then it has to be reinforced in every way possible, so an assessment system that emphasises the significance and centrality of deep learning is a prerequisite.

Other strategies that can help to secure the growth mindset approach include:

- Ensuring that everyone involved understands the underpinning theory and how the principles of a growth mindset apply to them personally.
- Developing a common growth mindset vocabulary to be used by everyone in the school.
- Senior leaders modelling using the growth mindset approach when praising learners.
- Focusing feedback on improvement strategies.
- Using peer coaching to reinforce the availability of feedback.
- Making sure the prevailing culture is one of work hard in order to improve.

How accurate and effective is the use of formative assessment in your school? Is there a clear correlation between assessment and progress?

For some schools, what has been described in this chapter will be familiar and will simply confirm 'work in progress'. For other schools, these ideas will seem naive if not unrealistically utopian. However, if the majority of schools actually read what they say in their aims and values or mission statement, then what has been described here will, in fact, provide the means to translate those aspirations into practice. The movement towards a truly learning-centred school is complex and fraught with compromises, but there are some very positive steps that can be taken, even in a system that prioritises shallow, quantifiable outcomes over the creation of shared understanding. In particular, there are practical innovations that will begin to help shift the culture of the school:

- Moving towards personalisation by developing individual learning plans for all pupils, and building in real choices to what is learnt and how learning takes place.
- Recognising the importance of relationships by changing the layout of classrooms and working on the emotional literacy of all aspects of school life.
- Using social media to build learning relationships across the community.
- Working towards the thinking school by involving every member of the school community in learning how to think.
- Recognising the centrality of developing memory, challenge and practice in every aspect of learning and teaching by embedding them into all school activities.
- Working to develop a community focused on growth mindsets.
- Appreciating that formative assessment is the best preparation for summative assessment.

Learning as the core purpose of school leadership

Classify each of the following components of your leadership of change as A, B, C or D, according to the extent to which it shows:

A. High confidence and is well established in principle and practice.

B. Emergent practice for some of the time.

C. Some awareness but no consistent practice.

D. No awareness.

Leadership behaviours	**Rating/ evidence**	**Implications/ action**
Confident understanding of the impact of leadership on the quality of learning		
Providing a curriculum model that integrates content and process		
Creating a culture that starts with the dignity and uniqueness of each learner		
Developing a culture based on high levels of emotional literacy		
Recognising the totality of the learning experience and securing high levels of engagement		
Recognising the plasticity of intelligence and securing appropriate cognitive interventions		
Making appropriate use of the evidence from neurological research		
Modelling the behaviours and language appropriate to a growth mindset		
Ensuring consistency in assessment that focuses on understanding		

Chapter 5

Leading through collaboration and cooperation

One of the key trends in school leadership is the movement from autonomous working to collaboration in order to address the main barriers to closing the gap. It could be that the best way to secure sustainable improvement is to enhance the level of collaborative working both between schools and between schools and the wider community. This approach leads to the following questions:

- How far is leadership based on cooperation and collaboration?
- How challenging is the move from autonomy to collaborative working?
- What contribution does the school make to developing social capital across the community?
- How comfortable are you with the concept of leadership beyond the school – that is, system leadership?
- How comfortable are you with the idea of intervention – that is, preventing failure rather than putting things right?

The variables influencing educational success

A significant majority of children in many developed education systems enjoy lives with high levels of well-being, educational success and positive life chances. They attend good schools and experience a wide range of educational successes. However, in a significant number of education systems there is a significant minority who do not enjoy these advantages. Worryingly, almost without exception, these are children who are also the most vulnerable and disadvantaged in social, cultural and economic terms. In many countries (e.g. England, the United States, New Zealand), there is a real issue with the lack of equity in the system. This is often described as 'the gap' or 'the long tail of underachievement'. There is equality when every child's right to go to school is secured; however, there is no equity when there is no guarantee that every child will go to a good school. Even in a good school, there is no guarantee that there will be consistently effective teaching and learning, especially for the most vulnerable.

Historically, the response to the imperative to narrow or close the gap has been to focus on the individual school and to introduce strategies broadly conceived around the model of school improvement. This has usually taken the form of support and/or external intervention. But, in general, school improvement has been an essentially internal process – that is, supported self-improvement. There is no doubt that this works, but it often takes a significant amount of time, it is highly demanding on internal capacity and it may not be sustainable.

The central proposition in this chapter is that perhaps we've got it the wrong way round. Instead of focusing on school improvement, maybe we should be focusing, firstly, on the school's social context and, secondly, looking to collaborative relationships as having a greater potential to secure enduring improvement. This would mean that school leadership would have to change its horizons. In *More Than the Sum*, the Audit Commission (2006: 4) came to the conclusion that:

> School improvement and renewal are inseparable issues from neighbourhood improvement and renewal, particularly in the most disadvantaged areas. While schools are profoundly affected by their

> neighbourhoods, they equally have a key role in promoting cohesion and building social capital.

From this perspective, the overarching influence is a student's social context. School factors, notably the quality of teaching and learning, are significant but are subordinate to social, cultural and economic factors. For some this leads to a very clear conclusion:

> schools can – and should – be charged with narrowing educational inequality. However, a focus on general school improvement policies will not be sufficient to do the job. (Clifton and Cook 2012: 5)

This perspective leads us to two important points. Firstly, school leaders may need to engage with issues that are beyond the school's normal remit – that is, the social and economic factors which influence the educational opportunities available to children and young people. Secondly, it might be that the demands of securing equity across the system are too much to be dealt with by schools working on their own. Both these perspectives have an obvious implication: the historic boundaries of school leadership (i.e. the school itself) may have to be broadened to include intervention in social issues and active collaboration with other schools:

> At present, the tragedy of school change is that only about 30 per cent of the explanation for variations in school achievement appears to be attributable to factors in the school ... Perhaps it is now time for leaders to lead their schools and exert their influence far beyond the school walls. (Moreno et al. 2007: 5)

'Perhaps it is now time for leaders to lead their schools and exert their influence far beyond the school walls.' On the basis of the evidence offered and the opinions presented, how do you respond to Moreno's exhortation?

What do you see as the compelling arguments for change and the possibly equally compelling case for the status quo?

It might be helpful to think in terms of personal mind maps and the extent to which people have a clearly defined area of personal confidence connected to a sense of control and familiarity – our personal territory. Moving beyond our normal range of responsibilities and self-confidence is always challenging.

The school in context – the key factors

Although there are some very distinguished examples of schools having a transformational impact on the achievement of young people from a range of disadvantaged backgrounds, scaling this up across an entire society is problematic. However, doing so might have a greater impact on securing equity than the remorseless focus on improving schools, which, as Figure 5.1 shows, has a relatively limited overall impact.

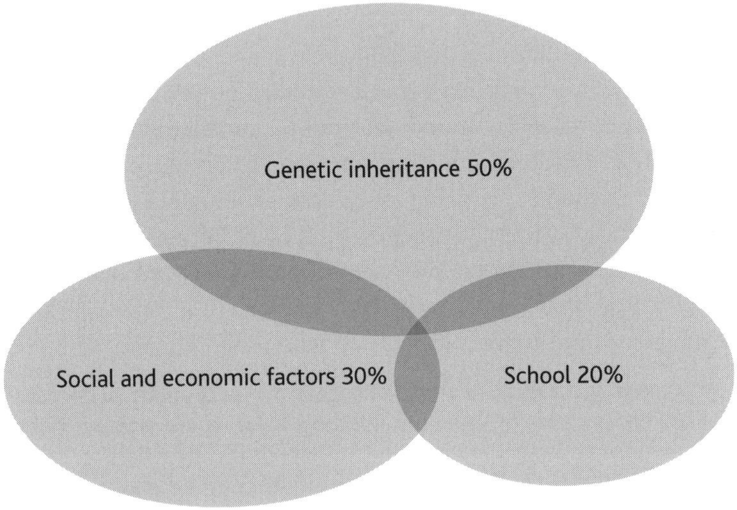

Figure 5.1. The variables influencing educational success

There is much political and conceptual debate about the relative significance and impact of social, contextual and school-based variables. The school improvement perspective has tended to focus on the school itself as the primary source of improvement. Alternative perspectives recognise the importance of the school but place significant stress on socio-economic factors, arguing that in terms of well-being, life chances and social success, it is these factors that will outweigh, and often explain, the success of school-based approaches. Three broad conclusions seem to emerge from the research analysing the factors influencing student learning:

> First, student background characteristics – especially social, economic and cultural background – frequently emerge as the most important source of variation in student achievement. ...
>
> Second, school-related factors explain a smaller part of the variations in student learning than student characteristics.
>
> Thirdly, at the school level the factors that are closest to student learning, such as teacher quality and classroom practices, tend to have the strongest impact on student achievement. (Pont et al. 2008: 33)

There is no consensus about the relative significance of the three variables in Figure 5.1. For some years, there has been a general acceptance of the 80:20 (or 70:30) rule to explain the ratio of social effects to school effects, although the precise relationship is contested. We now need to add in a major element – the cognitive potential of the individual child based on their genes.

The emerging critique of prevailing assumptions about the nature of the learning process has been substantially deepened by the publication of research carried out by Robert Plomin and his colleagues into the genetic influences on academic performance. The significant finding has been that differences in educational achievement at GCSE level are not primarily an indication of the quality of teachers or schools, and nor are they attributable to family factors. The research indicates that the variance within GCSE scores is attributable to genetics, and not to the school or family environment. Children are not blank slates, so we need to start by recognising and respecting the learner as a unique human being. This is not about biological determinism – any debate about our genetic inheritance is as much about nurture as nature. Asbury and Plomin (2014: 162) make it quite clear that it is about respect for the individual and targeted interventions:

> Children who find mastery of skills difficult are, in almost all cases, not genetically distinct from other children. There is no genetic reason why they cannot succeed given personalized support.

Securing equity may, therefore, be very much a matter of responding to the needs of each learner in a way that goes far beyond differentiation and actually starts with the uniqueness of each learner. This would seem to require a profound change in our schools.

Does your personal experience and understanding confirm or challenge the ratios set out in Figure 5.1?

If the model is broadly accurate, then what are the implications for the policies and strategies used to close the gap in your school?

How does your use of the pupil premium reflect the ratios in Figure 5.1?

The second set of significant variables explores the impact of the child's social and economic context. There seems little doubt that the success of an individual child at school is determined to a highly significant extent by factors that are outside the school's control:

> The picture so far is that the circumstances in which children are born and grow have a profound effect on what happens to them in school. …
>
> To achieve good educational results, we also need action to reduce poverty and socio-economic inequality and to improve the family and community context in which children's education will take place. (Marmot 2015: 169)

Personal well-being and high social capital appear to be non-negotiable preconditions for educational success. Across England, it is possible to identify a direct correlation between areas of high well-being and high social capital with areas of high academic performance and educational success. Equally, it is possible to demonstrate that the relative performance of different national educational systems is also correlated with social effects. Young people perform better by a range of criteria, but especially in terms of academic attainment, in communities and countries where:

- There is effective parenting and high quality family life.
- Children grow up in a secure and effective community.
- The potential impact of social class is minimised.
- The impact of poverty is mitigated.

Of course, there are very distinguished exceptions to this broad rule but the relationship seems to be persistent and pervasive. While schools can make a difference, the social variables and the interaction of nature and nurture on an individual's genetic inheritance make a bigger difference.

Putnam (2000: 154) is robust about the impact of social capital:

> child development is powerfully shaped by social capital ... trust, networks, and norms of reciprocity within a child's family, school, peer group, and larger community have wide-ranging effects on the child's opportunities and choices and, hence, on behaviour and development.

In his most recent work, Putnam (2015: 111) is unequivocal in identifying the potential for positive and negative outcomes from family life:

> So on the positive side of the ledger, the child's interaction with caring responsive adults is an essential ingredient in successful development. On the other side of the ledger, neglect and stress, including what is now called 'toxic stress' can impede successful development. Chronic neglect, in fact, is often associated with a wider range of developmental consequences than is overt physical abuse. Beating kids is bad, but entirely ignoring them can be even worse.

To these perspectives can be added a range of more specific factors as well as the potential implications of the interaction of multiple negative aspects. In one of the most substantial studies of disadvantaged and vulnerable young people, Sabates and Dex (2012) identify the 10 most significant risk factors influencing the well-being and life chances of children and young people. Across Britain, using their model of social disadvantage, about 40 per cent of children experience no risks, 30 per cent one risk, 14 per cent two risks, 7 per cent three risks, 7 per cent four risks and 2 per cent more than five risks. (These figures lead to an interesting ratio of 70:30 in terms of the balance of children's well-being and their potential to thrive in the education system.) The impact of multiple risk factors is direct:

> children exposed to two or more risks were likely to have higher average negative outcomes on all dimensions at age three and five than children exposed to fewer risks ... We can see a widening gap in cognitive development, hyperactivity, peer problems and prosocial behaviours for children with exposure to two or more risks compared to one or no risks between ages three and five. (Sabates and Dex 2012: 18)

The school is a necessary but not sufficient variable in a child's potential to thrive and succeed – and, in some respects, is the most open to influence and change. A change of leadership in a school can lead to very dramatic improvements in behaviour and the quality of teaching and learning. However, the other key variables – poverty, social class, parenting and family life and the quality of community engagement – can be addressed with varying degrees of potential impact by schools, but only if the role of the school is radically reappraised.

Another way of understanding this issue is to consider the implications of the very simple fact that children spend only 16 per cent of their lives each year in school. While that 16 per cent is disproportionately significant, it would be naive in the extreme to pretend that the school can function hermetically sealed off from the community it serves. It is similarly fallacious to argue that 'You go to school to learn' or 'If you don't behave you won't learn'. Children and young people are never not learning – misbehaving is often one of the most powerful learning experiences.

Children on free school meals continue to underachieve in the classroom, regardless of whether the school they attend is rated highly by Ofsted or not. Professor Steve Strand of Oxford University states that the stubbornness of the attainment gap across all types of schools suggests that the quality of a school is not enough to overcome a disadvantaged background. His research (Strand 2014) challenges the current narrative favoured by politicians of all parties – that improving a school's Ofsted status will close the gap. Instead, he suggests that factors outside school, rather than anything happening in the classroom, may be the root cause of attainment gaps.

> According to Strand's research, the gap in performance at GCSE between free school meal and non-free school meal students in outstanding schools is 25 per cent, in good schools it is also 25 per cent and in schools requiring improvement it is 22 per cent. Good and outstanding schools may raise the bar for pupils but they do not close the gap. What are the implications of this finding for our understanding of what constitutes good, outstanding and excellent in how schools are judged?

Traditional school improvement does not really address the issue of the lack of equity; in fact, in some respects it exacerbates it. Hutchings and his colleagues are very clear on this point:

> On closing the gap, sponsor academies are doing better than all mainstream schools and converter academies (with standalone academies having the narrowest gaps) but this may reflect (a) relative low achievement across the board in the academies concerned (this is shown to

> be the case for the majority of chains in our sample), and/or (b) the demographic of sponsor academies which tend to contain more young people that are working class, if not on free school meals. (Hutchings et al. 2015: 41)

The problem of how to close the gap and secure equity is further reinforced in a study by the Social Mobility and Child Poverty Commission, *Chain Effects 2015*, on the impact of academisation:

> Children from less advantaged family backgrounds who were high attaining in early cognitive skill assessments are found to be less able or at least less successful at converting this early high potential into career success. (McKnight 2015: iii)

Parents with relative economic security or higher social class are more successful at ensuring that their children who demonstrate academic ability at an early age translate this potential into academic success and employability in adulthood. They use the same approach with their early low attaining children – resources and strategies which are simply not available to less advantaged families to the same extent. Thus, it seems that neither the legal status of a school nor its performance according to Ofsted are actually making any impact on the gap. Edgar (2001: 160) summarises the central issue:

> Because human and social capital develop within families and through wider social networks, our schools must be reconceptualised as just one part of the learning culture, and become embedded in society in new ways.

This means that schools can become active agents in their communities and, pivotally, key mechanisms in securing high social capital and social change. Schools thus engage with literacy across the community, provide family support workers and psychiatric nurses and make the school a community resource in order to address the causes of early disadvantage. The underlying principle here is 'predict and prevent' rather than 'find and fix'. Early intervention is more effective, more cost efficient and more equitable than working to put things right, but it may well require a fundamental shift in social and political attitudes and a willingness to recognise that sustainable changes in a community need to be embedded in norms, expectations and culture. Prescription is not enough; the patient will only recover with a change in lifestyle which is rooted in a changed sense of self and the possibility of hope.

> It is beyond doubt that poverty and marginalisation impact on levels of achievement and that substantially higher resources are needed to enable schools in more troubled areas to respond to social distress and disruptive relationships. At the same time, raising aspirations is a political question [that] requires a conscious rejection of deficit thinking about students and their families. (Wrigley et al. 2012: 201)

> To what extent does the evidence presented in this section point to the need for new models of collaboration between schools and families, the wider community and all the agencies concerned with the well-being of children and young people?

Collaboration and cooperation

We collaborate in order to create a community – the success of any community is contingent on the depth and integrity of the cooperation. The more successful we are at learning to cooperate, the more likely it is that we will achieve a depth of collaboration that supports the promise of living and working in a community.

One of the key ways of understanding what is often described as the 'human side of enterprise' is viewing social interaction in terms of bonding or bridging – in essence, the extent to which we are inclined to engage or disengage with each other (i.e. the extent of collaboration). The underpinning concept here is social capital – the nature and quality of social interactions and the relative levels and integrity of relationships, networks and trust.

Bonding social capital defines the extent to which a community has internal integrity and coherence, while bridging social capital defines the extent to which a community is willing to engage with other communities. This perspective might be best understood in terms of collaboration within boundaries or horizons. Do we collaborate within our own community (bonding), or are we able and willing to collaborate with other communities (bridging)?

The bonding community is essentially introvert – usually for very good reason. Conversely, the bridging community is essentially extrovert

– confident in working beyond its own boundaries, inclusive and favouring interdependence as a preferred mode of functioning. Healthy and mature communities tend to be confident and secure in their own identity and so are able to engage with other communities.

Bonding – Autonomy	Bridging – Interdependency
Inward looking	Outward looking
Potentially exclusive	Inclusive
Self-reinforcing and legitimating	Pluralist and consensual
Homogeneous	Heterogeneous

Table 5.1. The characteristics of bonding and bridging communities

The differences between bonding and bridging communities are well illustrated by Saxenian in her study of two centres of the IT industry in the United States – Silicon Valley and Route 128. She describes Route 128 as being:

> based on independent firms that internalise a wide range of productive activities. Practices of secrecy and corporate loyalty govern relations ... hierarchies ensure that authority remains centralised and information tends to flow vertically. The boundaries between and within firms and between firms and local institutions thus remain ... distinct. (Saxenian 1996: 3).

Silicon Valley, in contrast, works by being:

> a regional network-based industrial system that promotes collective learning and flexible adjustment among specialist producers of a complex of related technologies. The region's dense social networks and open labour markets encourage experimentation and entrepreneurship. (Saxenian 1996: 2)

The implications of a bonding or bridging culture in terms of relative success are self-evident in this example.

In his discussion of the factors that influenced the disastrous collapse of the astonishing civilisation of Easter Island, Diamond (2005: 119) suggests that an important element was, 'a focus on statue construction ... and competition between the clans and chiefs driving the erection of bigger statues'. The combination of bonding and competition led to the collapse of what had been a sophisticated and very successful civilisation – not that this would ever happen in a 21st century education system.

These are not direct analogies, but there may be an issue in education in terms of the tension between bonding and bridging and, in particular, autonomy and collaboration. In many ways, one of the outcomes of the school improvement movement has been an emphasis on the autonomous school. There now seems little doubt that a strong sense of corporate identity is a necessary prerequisite to sustainable improvement. Schools in England are held accountable as self-directed, autonomous institutions, but the drift towards the marketisation of educational provision reinforces the imperative towards bonding. Yet this seems to fly in the face of what we know about human advancement.

We have improved and evolved through collaboration. In fact, cooperation is essential to human progress and the failure to cooperate is usually the basis for social decay. Effective leadership has to recognise that:

> We are traders in ideas, goods, favors and information and not simply the competitors that traditional market thinking would make us. In each area of our lives we develop a network of trusted relationships and favor those ties over others. Exchanges within this network of trusted social ties facilitate idea flow, creating an inclusive, vigorous culture and are responsible for the collective intelligence of our society. (Pentland 2014: 130)

The challenge for leaders is to achieve appropriate levels of cooperation and collaboration both within the community and between communities. Even in the smallest school, bonding cannot be assumed and, paradoxically, the greater the level of bonding, the greater the potential challenge to bridging. But this does not mean that the two are necessarily mutually exclusive:

> In this respect swarms in nature have taught us two lessons. The first is that, by working together in smart groups, we too can lessen the impact of uncertainty, complexity and change. ...
>
> The second lesson of smart swarms is that we don't have to surrender our individuality. In nature, good decision making comes as much from competition as from compromise, from disagreement as much as from consensus. (Miller 2010: 267)

What is the case, and this applies as much to effective learning as to leadership, is that the vast majority of human beings spend much of their time working collaboratively and interdependently:

> Whether designing an airplane, assembling a motorcycle, or analysing the human genome, the ability to integrate the talents of dispersed individuals and organizations has become *the* defining competency for managers and firms. (Tapscott and Williams 2006: 18)

Is your school a Route 128 school or a Silicon Valley school?

In which context do you feel most psychologically comfortable?

What are the perceptions and expectations of your pupils, their parents, the governing body and the staff?

What, for you, is the appropriate balance in terms of bonding and bridging for a high performance school?

Bonding: the school as a cooperative community

De Geus (1997: 9) stresses the importance of what might be seen as the human side of organisational life – the centrality of relationships and the pivotal importance of a sense of community:

> To put it another way: companies die because their managers focus on the economic activity of producing goods and services, and they forget that their organization's true nature is that of a community of humans.

It might be that the performance culture which increasingly dominates all aspects of corporate life has had a negative impact on the social nature of schools. It might be that the sense of community has been eroded by the imperative of producing 'goods and services' and focusing on narrowly defined outcomes.

If education is about more than quantitative outcomes at Key Stages 2 and 4, it might be that we need to extend and enhance our focus on the well-being of the individual in the community, which is what every school aspires to do but finds that systems and structures may conspire against it. From this perspective, it might be appropriate to take the view of community espoused by Archbishop Desmond Tutu in his discussion of the southern African concept of ubuntu:

> We don't come fully formed into the world. We learn how to think, how to walk, how to speak, how to behave, indeed how to be human from other human beings. We need other human beings in order to be human. We are made for togetherness ... to exist in a tender network of interdependence. That is how you have ubuntu – you care, you are hospitable, you're gentle, you're compassionate and concerned. (Battle 1997: 35)

Ubuntu is variously interpreted, but perhaps the most compelling version is, 'I am because we are'. Tutu makes the point that it is through community that we develop our full potential as human beings – what better argument for schools to become communities? There is a great deal of evidence to show that there are a range of benefits from living in an effective community:

- People with good networks of relationships have fewer mental problems.
- Individuals recover faster from illness, smoke less and live longer.
- Individuals are less likely to commit crime or to be the victim of crime.
- Children have higher levels of well-being.
- Children are more likely to successfully complete their education.
- Divorce rates are likely to be lower.
- Rates of substance abuse are likely to be lower.

As Putnam (2000: 326) argues:

> social connectedness is one of the most powerful determinants of our well-being. The more integrated we are with our community, the less likely we are to experience colds, heart attacks, strokes, cancer, depression, and premature death of all sorts.

In this chapter, we have argued that in order to secure effective learning for all, it might be necessary to rethink the nature of the school and rethink the context for learning. There is compelling evidence that living and working in a genuine community is one of the most beneficial social arrangements for human beings. If this is true, then perhaps schools should be functioning communities in microcosm and model the way in which they work so that pupils learn how to live in a community. To become good citizens young people need to practise democracy as a way of life. To become members of a community they need to grow up in an effective community.

Malcolm Gladwell provides one of the most compelling accounts of an effective community in his book *Outliers* (2008). He describes the Italian immigrant community of Roseto in Pennsylvania, which was one of the healthiest in the United States. Roseto became famous in the 1950s when it emerged that it was effectively free of heart disease and almost all other chronic illnesses. The people of Roseto were not healthy because of their diet but 'because of where they were from, because of the world they had created for themselves in their tiny little town in the hills' (Gladwell 2008: 7). To understand why Roseto was so successful, the researchers had to 'look beyond the individual':

> They had to understand the culture he or she was part of, and who their families and friends were. They had to appreciate the idea that the values of the world we inhabit and the people we surround ourselves with have a profound effect on who we are. (Gladwell 2008: 9)

The people of Roseto were physically healthy because they were socially healthy, and they were socially healthy because they lived in an effective community. It is possible that they were healthier because they were happier – which seems to be an entirely appropriate model on which to base the education of children. Circumstances appear to be even more propitious in Sardinia:

> In Sardinia 10 times as many men live past 100 than the average ... a sense of inclusion turned out to be a crucial piece of the longevity puzzle. Every centenarian we met was supported by kith and kin, visitors who stopped to chat, bring food and gossip, provide personal care, a kiss on the cheek.
>
> Our survival hinges on social interaction, and that is not only true of the murky evolutionary past ... social integration – the feeling of being part of a cohesive group – fosters immunity and resilience. (Pinker 2015: 57)

There is also a very high correlation between living in an effective community and high social capital, well-being, enhanced life chances and educational success. One of the factors that explains the success of some independent schools is the very powerful sense of community and belonging they create. If the school is an authentic community in its own right, and if it provides authentic experiences for its pupils and their parents, then there is surely the possibility that the school will help to influence the community that it serves.

There are numerous formulations for an effective community. The type of community and its context will always determine the particular set of permutations; however, for most purposes, the following factors would seem to be relevant:

- Shared values and norms that actively inform day-to-day life.
- A strong community identity and a sense of place.
- Positive social relationships, high trust and a sense of interdependence.
- Open communication based on a shared language.
- A sense of equity and fairness.

Does your school meet these criteria for an effective community?

Does the community your school serves meet these criteria?

To what extent is your school an agent for social change?

Bridging: improvement through collaboration

Bonding is a very powerful social, psychological, political and emotional imperative. We like to feel part of something and we need to express our sense of belonging in a wide variety of ways – not least of which is resisting any movement to engage with those who might be seen as possible rivals. As we demonstrated in the previous section, collaboration within schools cannot be taken for granted so, equally, it would be wrong to assume that collaboration between schools is a self-evident good. However, the evidence seems to be compelling:

> There are common sense and pragmatic reasons for schools' collaboration in learning networks to achieve transformation ... collaboration across schools is a necessity rather than an optional extra in the transformation project. (Desforges 2004: 2)

The evidence base supporting collaboration seems to be robust and highly credible. Crucially, there does not seem to be any significant data against collaboration. Indeed:

> There is evidence that the process of change is more resilient and improvement more sustainable when schools collaborate and learn from other schools. Schools that sustain improvement are usually well networked and have a good structure of internal support. (Leithwood et al. 2010: 238)

Collaboration might well be one of the missing ingredients as far as successful school improvement is concerned. Leithwood goes on to point out that collaboration can be mutually beneficial and that collaboration is not necessarily an altruistic act, but rather one that has the potential to enhance the effectiveness of both donor and recipient. Fullan (2010: 75) is persuasive on this particular perspective:

> The power of collective capacity is that it enables ordinary people to accomplish extraordinary things – for two reasons. One is that knowledge about effective practice becomes more widely available and accessible on a daily basis. The second reason is more powerful still – working together generates commitment.

One example that seems to vindicate Fullan's optimism is evidence emerging from the evaluation of London Challenge. One of the key variables that explains the success of the London Challenge initiative has been described in the following terms:

> Within and outside London Challenge there was a widespread view that 'system leaders' had a responsibility that went beyond the individual institution where they were currently working ... system leaders accepted that they had a shared and collective responsibility with other school leaders for the well-being of all students in their community. (Baars et al. 2014: 13)

What is very clear is that, in a range of contexts, it is the introduction of some form of collaborative relationship that can enhance both the potential impact of an improvement strategy and its sustainability. This is a pivotal insight that has been reinforced by the findings of the House of Commons Committee on Education:

> School partnerships and cooperation have become an increasingly important part of a self-improving or school-led system. We believe that such collaboration has great potential to continue driving improvement to the English education system.
>
> School collaboration offers benefits to all schools involved. While there are tensions between competition and collaboration, these are largely creative tensions and collaboration is growing in many forms within a competitive school system. (Education Select Committee 2013)

It is the latter point that captures the essence of the debate around bridging and bonding: a culture that is based on bonding will have a predisposition towards competition as a way of reinforcing and consolidating its integrity and autonomy. Bridging, by contrast, is almost always symbiotic with cooperation and collaboration, although there will be a spectrum of degrees of engagement.

It would be naive to minimise the power of bonding and the aspirational nature of bridging – local politics and very real issues around the viability and integrity of organisations will always be key determinants of levels of engagement. However, bridging and bonding can be reconciled and work to their mutual enhancement:

> Our experience and evidence of exceptional organizations makes it clear that just as collaboration and competition can no longer be neatly separated from each other, neither can the ways of combining them. There are many strategic benefits from joining together collaborative and competitive intent, from aligning joint effort, and for combining collective investment for competitive gain. (Hargreaves et al. 2014: 91)

As Hargreaves and his colleagues point out, the relationship between collaboration and competition does not have to be a zero-sum game – there does not have to be a winner. They introduce the concept of 'co-opetition' – cooperating with a competitor to mutual benefit. It is sometimes difficult to appreciate just how much the idea of the zero-sum game dominates educational policymaking. The importance of winning is fundamental to so many aspects of how school leaders think, so it is hardly surprising that collaboration can seem utterly inappropriate.

One way of understanding the relationship between collaboration and competition is to see them as part of a continuum related to institutional autonomy or collaboration (see Figure 5.2) – what might be described as degrees of engagement.

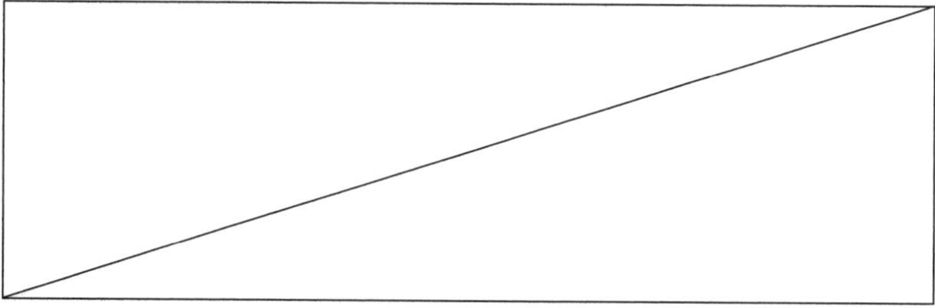

1. Autonomy 2. Competition 3. Co-opetition 4. Interdependence 5. Collaboration

Figure 5.2. The movement from autonomy to collaboration

1. Highly autonomous with only functional relationships with other schools (e.g. partner primary schools – but probably referred to as 'feeder schools'!). Some degree of liaison on a geographical basis, loose networks.
2. Some degree of engagement through local partnerships (e.g. a teaching school alliance) but only limited sharing of resources. Support based on 'good neighbourliness'.
3. Regular engagement and sharing of resources, liaison over local issues, shared CPD and regular interaction. Active collaboration (e.g. shared sixth form) but with a positive culture of cooperation and competition as found in Silicon Valley: 'Companies compete intensely while at the same time learning from one another about changing markets and technologies through informal communication and collaborative practices' (Saxenian 1996: 2).
4. Legal basis for the relationship. Formal commitment to collaborative working and system leadership (e.g. executive principal) but schools preserving individual identities.
5. Fully integrated with a high level of interdependent working reinforced through formal contractual relationships (e.g. trust status, working as a federation or chain). Common policies, sharing of resources and staff. System leadership and strategic planning.

On the basis of the range of sources referred to in this chapter, it becomes possible to offer a rationale for collaboration based on the perceived benefits to both individuals and the wider community:

- Collaboration has the potential to significantly enhance the impact of school improvement strategies and to maximise their leverage.
- The creation of communities of schools is more likely to lead to authentic equity and inclusion as principles are reinforced through collaborative planning and practice.
- Consistent practice is more attainable through shared CPD, benchmarking and peer monitoring and review.
- Professional practice is more likely to be shared, embedded and sustained through opportunities for collaborative learning (e.g. joint practice development), research, networking, modelling, adopting and adapting.
- Collaboration builds social capital through effective communication, networking and trust.
- Innovation, creativity and risk taking are more likely to flourish in a collaborative environment – the wheel is less likely to be reinvented.
- Collaborative structures have the potential to facilitate greater flexibility in the deployment of teachers and leaders, and so disseminate quality practice and maximise the impact of the most effective professionals.
- In a time of economic stringency, collaborative strategies may offer benefits in terms of economies of scale and securing more for less.

A list like this will clearly be prioritised in different ways in different contexts and at different times. However, it would be dangerous to assume that such a list has any value or strength except through the perceptions of those involved. The benefits of collaboration will always be subjective, in the same way that collaboration only really works through informal relationships rather than formal policies and strategies:

> collaborative cultures do require attention to the structures and formal organization of school life, but their underlying sources of strength are informal in relationships, conversation, expressions of interest, provisions of support, and ultimately the mobilization of collective expertise

> and commitment ... Talk together, plan together, work together – that's the simple key. (Hargreaves and Fullan 2012: 114)

Is there a culture of collaboration working within your school? What examples would you offer to demonstrate your school's commitment to collaborative working with other schools and agencies?

Leadership for collaboration

There seems little doubt that leadership of an autonomous institution with a traditional hierarchical structure, clear division of labour and well-defined and logical bureaucratic procedures is much easier than leadership of a complex collaborative network or a community. There is already some evidence that moving from being head teacher of an autonomous school to an executive principal or chief executive role is potentially very challenging. 'Leadership beyond the school' is not just a matter of extending traditional leadership styles and strategies into a wider context; it requires a basic rethink of certain key assumptions. Leadership to enable effective collaboration and secure an authentic community may need to demonstrate a range of qualities, particularly given the propensity for autonomous working found in education. In this context, effective leadership has to be about engagement and connection:

> The best bosses understand and care about the social motivation of all members of the team. Bosses have to foster better connections between themselves and their team, among team members and between the team and other outside groups and individuals critical to success ... Creating this identification, this attachment to the group, is an essential component of successful leadership. (Lieberman 2013: 273–274)

There is another level of leadership emerging in some education systems that might be best described as that of the chief executive. Historically, most chief education officers in English local authorities started their careers as classroom teachers but usually made an early transfer to local government. There were examples of head teachers moving across but chief officers tended to be career education officers. The movement towards academies, and those academies working in a range of permutations of trusts and other combinations, has led to the emergence of executive principals and chief executive officers (the terminology used is not yet consistent).

At a superficial level, the major difference between a head teacher and a CEO is largely a matter of scale – some academy trusts are now larger than many local authorities. However, this is to ignore a number of important differences relating to identity, culture, performance and accountability:

- A key foundation for every trust and chain is a set of core values that provide clarity of purpose, moral commitment and a sense of corporate identity and uniqueness.
- The CEO has to provide the strategic vision for the trust – given the educational lifecycle of children, a 12–15 year time frame might be appropriate.
- The CEO is accountable for the trust's performance in terms of closing the gap and functioning effectively and efficiently as a company and a charity.
- Given the geography of many trusts, there is a need for a corporate culture ('the brand') which secures engagement and commitment. This is very much about ethos and language.
- The CEO has to establish working relationships that balance control (tight) and trust (loose) – perhaps intervention in inverse proportion to success – and, crucially, work for consistency in terms of successful practice within and across schools.
- The CEO negotiates with regional school commissioners, trustees, professional associations, local governing bodies, school leaders and staff and community representatives.
- The CEO collaborates with other trusts and developing partnerships across the educational system and other agencies.

The crucial distinction is one of corporate identity – the very term indicates a fundamental reorientation of practice.

The nature of effective relationships is dealt with in more detail in Chapters 6 and 7, but it is worth stressing the specific leadership qualities and strategies relevant to collaboration and community development:

- The cornerstone for any degree of leadership for collaboration is respect – an authentic recognition and acceptance of every individual on their own terms and in a spirit of inclusion and equity.
- Leadership in a complex environment requires moral confidence – the ability to act in a morally consistent way and to secure understanding of, and commitment to, shared values.
- Authentic collaboration requires a high degree of empathy – the ability to understand another person on their terms of reference rather than imposing one's own interpretation on others.
- Successful leadership in a collaborative or community setting depends on the ability to build networks and cultivate multiple relationships with many different degrees of engagement.
- It would be naive to pretend that shared values and common purpose are enough to secure high performance. Leadership in this context involves consensus building, negotiation, making alliances and responding to challenges with agreed policies and strategies.
- Collaborative leadership has to be democratic, both in terms of securing inclusive participation and working through transparent and agreed procedures and protocols.
- Above all, leadership for collaboration has to be authentic, trustworthy and rooted in personal and professional integrity.

Leading through collaboration and cooperation

Classify each of the following components of your leadership of change as A, B, C or D, according to the extent to which it shows:

A. High confidence and is well established in principle and practice.

B. Emergent practice for some of the time.

C. Some awareness but no consistent practice.

D. No awareness.

Leadership behaviours	Rating/ evidence	Implications/ action
A sense of moral responsibility for the system beyond the school		
Understanding the significance of social capital as a factor in organisational success		
Working to minimise the boundaries between school and the wider community		
Developing the school as a community		
Being committed to collaboration as a key vehicle for improvement		
Fostering a collaborative culture within the school		
Developing personal strategies to enable a culture of collaborative working		
Cultivating the leadership team as a model of collaborative working		
Building networks, partnerships and mutually supportive relationships		

Chapter 6

Building capacity – sharing leadership

One of the most significant challenges to prevailing orthodoxies in education is to question the essentially hierarchical and personal basis of leadership. Schools, like many other contemporary organisations, are effectively leader centric. Given the demands on schools, it might be that one response is to build leadership capacity – quantitatively and qualitatively. This chapter explores this issue from the following perspectives:

- Is leadership in your school about personal status or collective capacity?
- To what extent is your school leader centric?
- In what ways is the prevailing culture of your school moving from dependency to interdependency?
- What is being done in your school to build a culture of trust and empowerment?
- How is your school working to secure leadership capacity and sustainability?

Perspectives on leadership

School leadership in the Anglophone world has tended to combine two apparently contradictory elements: personal autonomy and personal accountability. The potential for tension is reflected in the possibly disproportionate focus on the role and status of principals and head teachers; a situation which is exacerbated by anecdotal evidence showing how a school's effectiveness can be significantly transformed by a change of leadership at the top. This is reflected in an increasing tendency to see replacing the head teacher as the most potent panacea for a school's ills. The emphasis on one role, and the disproportionate significance attributed to the leader, possibly places an undue burden on one individual and thereby diminishes the potential of other staff.

Schools tend to be leader-centric organisations with a management structure that is largely hierarchical with well-defined and rigorously observed gradations of authority and responsibility. The career structure of British school leaders is very much a progression towards choice, control, a very heavy workload and almost incessant demands on time and energy. It is worth speculating on the historic legacy of the head teacher syndrome in British education and those systems that have cultural affinity with the British system (or are caricatures of it). There seems little doubt that the legacy of the great public school headmasters and headmistresses of the nineteenth century (Buss, Beale, Thring, Arnold) still has echoes and resonances today, however faint. Equally, the common perception of school leaders still seems to be firmly embedded in the nineteenth century.

> What do you perceive to be the cultural and historic legacy of school leadership? To what extent, if any, does it inform roles, structures, relationships and outcomes in your school?
>
> Is it appropriate for an essentially 19th century model of organisational leadership to inform 21st century schools?

The focus on the head teacher or principal *qua* leader has many manifestations, but some of the most significant are found in what might be called the semiotics of leadership – for example, how the spaces occupied by a leader can be personalised and decorated, the opportunities leaders have to control their environment (e.g. car parking), the control that leaders have over the deployment of their time (in some schools this is often reinforced by a personal assistant) and the ability to take unilateral decisions. (There is scope for a major study on the semiotics of head teachers' offices – the position of the desk, if there is one, can provide a powerful clue as to the leadership style of the occupier.)

> What are the semiotics of your office? What explicit and implicit messages does your office send?
>
> Are there any subliminal messages about your leadership style (e.g. seating arrangements)?
>
> To what extent is your office a personal space?

Of course, there are enormous differences between the work of the head of a small rural primary school with a teaching commitment and the chief executive of a multi-academy trust. However, human organisations do seem to have a propensity to grow, and when this happens:

> layers of management increase in number, size and complexity as organisations grow larger, because managers need managing too ... a large part of a boss's job in a big firm is to keep an organisation from collapsing under the weight of its own complexity. (Ridley 2015: 224)

The real issue might be that, in fact, the leader-centric approach is no longer valid or appropriate. Perhaps we need to move away from a focus on the individual leader to a focus on leadership as a relationship, so that a school's culture and norms become more significant than the personal skills of its leader. The success of Finnish schools is probably primarily attributable to the strength of social and cultural norms rather than the influence of a leader, or even leadership, in general. It is interesting how some high performing school systems are much more cautious about the nature and role of leadership than in the Anglophone world. In Finland, school leaders belong to the same trade union as teachers and all leaders have a teaching commitment:

> Leaders do not see themselves as 'the boss' – nor are they perceived as such by the teachers. Relationships are not very hierarchical, and in schools it is often difficult to distinguish teachers from support staff. (Hargreaves et al. 2008: 83)

This perspective is reinforced by Sahlberg (2015: 127):

> Teachers rely on their leaders' vision and the principal understands and trusts teachers' work. Therefore leadership and management in Finnish schools are informal but effective.

In some school systems there is a very real danger that the technical-rational model of the organisation will be significantly exacerbated by leader-centric models:

> Thus a culture with prominent 'schizoid' characteristics attracts to positions of influence individuals who will help it ever further down the same path. And the increasing domination of life by both technology and bureaucracy helps to erode the more integrative modes of attention to people and things which might help us to resist the advances of technology and bureaucracy. (McGilchrist 2009: 408)

The role of the leader is not so much to be emotionally intelligent, but rather to espouse a culture centred on the primacy of human interaction that is not dependent on one person's behaviour, moods and potentially dysfunctional personality. This is to move from an immature model based on dependency to a mature model based on interdependent working towards equity grounded in the essential dignity and value of every individual. In other words, from leadership as personal status to leadership as collective capacity. This is the movement from the school as a crypto-organisation to the school as an authentic community. Nussbaum (2013: 382) reinforces the central importance of recognising the complexity of any form of human interaction:

> Political emotions are the real emotions of real people; because people are heterogeneous, having different opinions, histories, and personalities, they can be expected to love, mourn, laugh, and strive for justice in specific and personal ways.

The following table uses Taylor's (2004) concept of the social imaginary as a way of understanding the differences between a leader-centric society and one that is built on the idea of leadership as collective capacity. A social imaginary is best understood as the collective understanding of a community or society at a given time. In essence, it is the consensual view that informs attitudes, perceptions, policies and actions.

Existing social imaginary – leader centricity	Emerging social imaginary – leadership as collective capacity
Hierarchical silos	Systems, networks and communities
Closed systems	Open systems
Dependency	Interdependency
Leader power and control	Leaders enabling and facilitating
Leadership as personal status	Leadership as collective capacity
Leader driven	Community driven
Outcomes-based performance	Social justice
Top-down communication	Lateral communication
Declaration	Negotiation
Control	Trust
Organisation	Community
Manage information	Create knowledge

Table 6.1. Alternative perspectives on leadership

Of course, the world is never as neatly polarised as lists like this would seem to imply. The truth usually lies in different places for each element and time and context will change the relationship. There is also always a hint of caricature in setting one dimension in contradistinction to another. However, it is often our implicit assumptions that determine behaviours and practice, so it is worth making them explicit to fully understand our own behaviours and those of our closest colleagues.

> For each of the criteria listed in Table 6.1, consider where you would place yourself on a continuum (e.g. what is the ratio of control to trust, to what extent is your school an organisation or a community?).
>
> Why does your leadership have these particular characteristics, and what are the implications of your approach?
>
> It might be instructive and enlightening to ask your colleagues to complete the same exercise and compare perceptions.

It is vital that school leaders have resources to support their personal review and reflection, in order to develop an understanding of themselves as leaders. One dimension of highly effective people, and thereby effective leaders, is the extent to which they are reflective and aware of their impact on others. In many respects, leadership development might be seen as a process of clarifying and understanding:

> the ways people imagine their social existence, how they fit together with others, how things go on between them and their fellows, the expectations that are normally met, and the deeper normative notions and images that underlie these expectations. (Taylor 2004: 23)

There is a very well-developed understanding of the notions of shared and distributed leadership, although the differences between them are not always clear or explicit. Harris (2014: 41) identifies the following key elements of distributed leadership:

- Distributed leadership is concerned with building the capacity to innovate and change.
- Distributed leadership is inclusive and implies broad-based involvement in leadership practice.
- Distributed leadership does not mean that everybody leads but rather that everybody has the potential to lead at some time, depending on expertise and experience.
- Distributed leadership occurs in various patterns – there is no overall blueprint – it depends on the context but it requires planning and alignment.

- Distributed leadership requires high levels of trust and reciprocal learning.

This list provides a very powerful antidote to the idea of the hero-leader working through personal power and hierarchical structures. There is little doubt that even the smallest schools, of necessity, are actively engaged in distributed leadership approaches. However, there is another dimension to the debate about distributed and shared leadership. Distributed leadership is usually manifested as various levels of delegation in the school hierarchy. This is usually within the 'gift' of the head teacher and/or governors and senior staff – distributed implies a distributor. An alternative perspective would be to see leadership as a collective capacity and shared entitlement. In other words, leadership is a community resource that is expressed in a variety of ways according to need – that is, a shared and collective capacity that is based on consent and need rather than power and status.

A very high level of trust is required for this to work, which, in turn, points to a sophisticated culture of interdependence that implies a depth of social capital:

> When trust is extended, it breeds responsibility in return. Emulation and peer pressure regulate the system better than hierarchy ever could. Teams set their own objectives and they take pride in achieving them. (Laloux 2014: 82)

Leadership and trust

Of all the personal qualities of a leader, trust is probably the most important. It is difficult to envisage any aspect of leadership work that is not profoundly dependent on trust – indeed, it could be argued that it would be impossible for leaders to work without it. The absence of trust implies control, coercion and compulsion. While trust is a highly significant personal quality, it is also a key characteristic of organisations:

> trust is the hidden variable that affects everything. The reason it's hidden is that leaders aren't looking for it in the systems, processes, policies and frameworks that all the day-to-day behaviours hang on ... [they] fail at the Organizational Trust level by not designing and aligning systems that promote trust. (Covey 2006: 239)

Consider the extent to which trust is fundamental to the following roles and relationships:

- Ensuring consistency across the school.
- Leading innovation and change.
- Creating an interdependent supportive community.
- Developing confidence between parents and schools.
- Developing confidence between learners and teachers.
- Working with marginalised groups and families.
- Building learning relationships.
- Enabling creativity and risk-taking learning.
- Creating high performing teams.

> What concrete examples would you offer to demonstrate the extent to which a classroom or school is a high trust organisation?
>
> Does your own school meet these criteria?

In broad social terms, organisational trust is an elusive quality, and yet it is also seen as central to most definitions of what it means to live and work in society. In his detailed and systematic analysis of leadership, Bottery (2004: 121) stresses the centrality of trust to any debate about what we are seeking to create in terms of effective societies and communities:

> a happy, tolerant and healthy society depends upon the blossoming of trust relationships both within communities and between them ... If the first order values of a society are not economic, but personal, social and moral, then trust has to be seen as a first order value that should be promoted for its own sake.

Covey (2006: 19) is unambiguous about the status and role of trust in personal and organisational life:

> When trust is high, the dividend you receive is like a performance multiplier ... In a company, high trust materially improves communication, collaboration, execution, innovation ... In your personal life, high trust significantly improves your excitement, energy, passion, creativity and joy in your relationships.

Hargreaves and Fink (2006: 213–214) also emphasise the power and significance of trust:

> Trust is a resource. It creates and consolidates energy, commitment, and relationships. When trust is broken, people lessen their commitment and withdraw from relationships, and entropy abounds.

They describe trust as the 'connective tissue' that binds schools together, and this image helps to reinforce the importance of healthy networks – neural and social – to effective learning. In the final analysis, as de Waal (2009: 167) points out:

> Trust is the lubricant that makes a society run smoothly. If we had to test everyone all the time before doing something together, we'd never achieve anything.

In organisational terms, trust is perhaps best exemplified through shared leadership that involves the location of authority at the 'point of delivery'. The movement from personal power (based on control) to shared authority (based on trust) is a complex and challenging one. There are many psychological, cultural and historical imperatives that support and reinforce the tendency towards control. The issue is to move people (whether aged 5 (or under) or 50 (or over)) from dependency to interdependency through the process of building trust.

Immature	→	→	**Mature**
Personal power			Shared authority
Hierarchy			Teams
Low trust			High trust
Dependency			Interdependency
Control	Delegation	Empowerment	Subsidiarity

Figure 6.1. Moving the school from control to subsidiarity

- *Control*: This involves a rigid hierarchy with strong bureaucratic, mechanistic systems. Exercise of formal power. Top-down communications with little if any consultation – compliance is required in a culture of permission seeking. Many relationships are essentially parent–child. There is an emphasis on status, privilege and personal symbols of authority. Resources are allocated by top-down methods with limited engagement or involvement. Outcomes-based answerability.

- *Delegation*: Formal allocation of tasks, high level of responsibility, limited authority. Tasks and outcomes allocated. Limited negotiation. Strict accountability. Limited discretion or initiative. Some feedback and participation. Formal consultation. Resources subject to limited negotiation. Organisational design is based around functional units with a 'span of control'. There are high degrees of specialisation.
- *Empowerment*: Delegation of responsibility with commensurate authority to act. Support through training and coaching. Agreed levels of discretion. Significant participation in decision making with distributed accountability. There are often self-managing teams at this stage. The key responsibility of organisational leadership is to set the vision and purpose and then support their implementation.
- *Subsidiarity*: Federal structure, high levels of autonomy, localised decision making within an agreed context and control over resources. Relationships based on consent and engagement. Function of central leadership is to provide support and reinforce core values, vision and purpose. High levels of trust with shared accountability.

Figure 6.1 is perhaps best seen as a continuum with an almost infinite number of gradations. These are subject to movement back and forth but broadly demonstrate the movement from control to subsidiarity expressed through increasing levels of personal and organisational trust. An almost exact parallel is found in parenting. Younger adolescents may well require a degree of control in their lives but as they mature into young adults so, hopefully, the relationship with their parents changes to one of increasing trust and the relationship moves from immaturity to maturity.

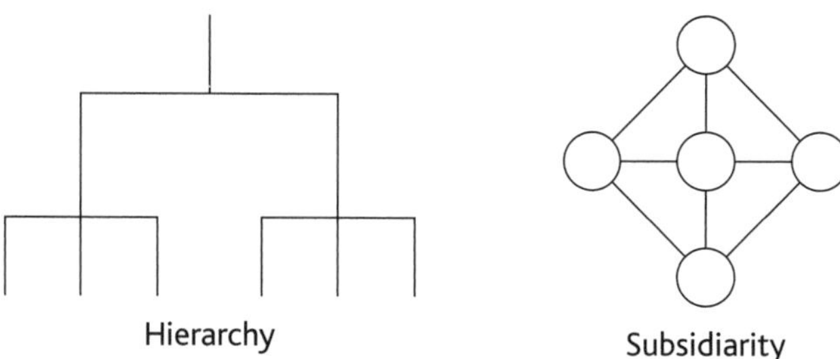

Figure 6.2. From hierarchy to subsidiarity

Figure 6.2 contrasts the traditional hierarchical organisational structure with what might be best described as the network structure that characterises subsidiarity. Most, but by no means all, businesses are best understood as hierarchies. Creative businesses often work as networks. Secondary schools are often hierarchical in nature; primary and, particularly, special schools often work as networks.

Leadership as personal status becomes shared authority as the school moves from immature control to mature subsidiarity. The traditional hierarchy of control found in almost all types of organisation in the Anglophone world is replaced by interdependent teams that balance shared values with degrees of autonomy. Subsidiarity might be best understood as federalism or a commonwealth in which decisions are taken at the lowest possible level, or closest to where they will have their effect, but with a very clear sense of shared values and common purpose as the integrating agents. This relates to the culture of the school as a whole, the relationships in teams and, most importantly, the relationships in classrooms and other learning environments. What is crucial is the recognition that trust is the result of learned experiences – that is, it is the product of choices made about relationships and working structures and processes.

Using Figures 6.1 and 6.2 as a starting point, what is the current level of organisational trust in your school?

The chances are that people and teams are spread across the control to subsidiarity model, but where do you feel the majority of staff cluster?

Would your senior colleagues agree with your diagnosis?

What are the implications for leadership in terms of relationships, processes and structures?

Teams in schools

One of the most effective ways of embedding organisational trust and securing structures and processes that reinforce a culture of high trust is to develop the organisation of the school in terms of self-managing teams. At its best, the self-managing team is a practical manifestation of high trust and a means of translating the rhetoric of subsidiarity into concrete practice. If form is to genuinely follow function, then the quasi-autonomous team as the basis of securing effective learning and positive relationships is probably the most powerful resource available.

> Team spirit is an inspiring and all pervading force that pulls and draws players together and upward – a feeling of excitement, energy and flow that infuses joy and exhilaration, bringing people to their peak. We find this kind of quality in a tight unit of highly capable and variable individuals that still acts as one body for a single cause, who will push each other forward as well as pull together. (Hargreaves et al. 2014: 106)

The concept of the team has long been seen as axiomatic to effective leadership. As soon as it is conceded that the leadership of an organisation is too big a job for one person, then the team becomes significant. However, in organisations such as schools, perhaps more so than in many other sectors, teams are more of a pious aspiration than a central social relationship. Genuine teams are rare in schools, although the label is freely applied – they are usually groups with pretensions.

A team is a group that meets a range of specific criteria (see Table 6.2). It is not enough to designate a group as a team, any more than the switch from 'senior management team' to 'leadership team' will lead to a significant change in working priorities or relationships. While labelling is important because language is a key determinant of culture, it is not enough. It might be argued that 'management team' is inherently paradoxical – teams are synonymous with the critical characteristics of effective leadership.

Groups	**Effective teams**
Pragmatic and essentially operational	Consensual values that inform practice
Diffuse purpose, multiple functions	Agreed core purpose and shared focus
Membership based on seniority or status	Membership that is fit for purpose – project-based teams
Formal relationships, no attempt to manage or improve interactions	High quality relationships and focus on processes
No sense of the team learning or commitment to collective development	Shared learning and collective development
No review and no recognition of the potential to enhance the quality of team working	Open review to secure improvement

Table 6.2. The difference between teams and groups

Schools are different to many organisations in the lack of flexibility they have to create teams. Many commercial organisations are designed around teams which are created for specific purposes and then disbanded. In such teams there is a very high correlation between the purpose of the team and its membership – that is, the team is designed to be 'fit for purpose'. Very often in schools, the membership of teams is determined by longevity and experience rather than aptitude and ability. Crucially, and for very understandable reasons, leadership teams invest very little in their own development – they are often task rather than process focused. Team leaders inherit their teams with little or no scope to change or develop the members. There are few opportunities for the team to grow as a team and limited time and space to explore potential or build capacity.

> Do you recognise your teams in the description of team spirit by Andy Hargreaves and his colleagues?
>
> Is your school made up of groups, emergent teams or genuinely self-managing teams?

The challenges facing schools require greater investment in the capacity and sustainability of their leadership. One person cannot possibility encompass all the knowledge, skills and qualities that organisations need to function. While the role of the leader remains pivotal, it may be that leadership in the organisation is best expressed through teams. This implies an acceptance of the concept of shared leadership; teams offer a powerful vehicle for putting this into effect.

If it is true that leadership behaviour is a crucial determinant of organisational culture and climate, then an effective leadership team would seem to be essential for the following reasons:

- It models best practice for the rest of the school.
- It maximises the leadership and management effectiveness of the leadership team.
- It enhances the potential of policies actually making an impact.
- It demonstrates, in a real way, the school's commitment to the development of every individual.
- It models effective learning and professional development.
- It offers the potential for greater creativity and better utilisation of skills and knowledge.
- It demonstrates commitment to personal well-being and the psychological health of the school.

In essence, the leadership team has to exemplify all that the organisation aspires to be. It has to model, demonstrate and exemplify the values and vision so that others can understand how principle is translated into practice. This is a highly challenging remit – a counsel of perfection – but it is also pragmatic: if the leadership team does not convert the abstract into the concrete, who else will? If there is an effective leadership team in an organisation, then there is the possibility of creating other teams throughout that organisation.

The effective leadership team needs to develop criteria for its own effectiveness and consider which of the components in Figure 6.3 are relevant and appropriate to its particular situation. Indeed, one of the key characteristics of the effective team is that it devotes time to establishing its own working protocols and criteria for effectiveness. This, of itself, is a powerful team development exercise and a source of consensus building and learning.

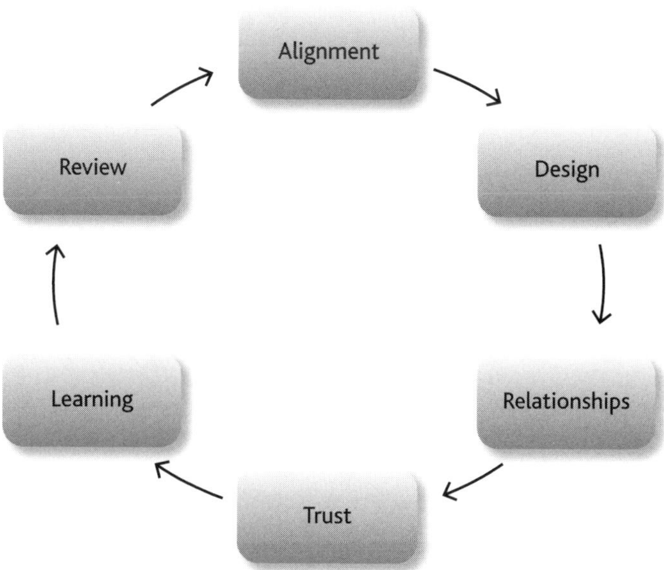

Figure 6.3. The six components of a high performing team

- *Alignment*: The team has to develop a common sense of values and vision which will act as the keystone to its activities. Meetings need to regularly revisit the core principles of the organisation to ensure that they are values-driven. There needs to be high consensus in the team – not a spurious 'collective responsibility' or an all-embracing hegemony – that is, a clear and shared sense of purpose which is known, understood and articulated. The effective team is also transparent about the principles by which it will achieve its purpose; it has a shared sense of internal and external accountability, responsibility to each member of the team and those that the team exists to serve.

- *Design*: The team needs an appropriate balance of types and behaviours. Belbin's team styles inventory (Belbin 1981) remains a useful model to explore the dynamics of the team in terms of team roles rather than organisational roles. Depending on the specific tasks, a team needs a portfolio of behavioural types:

    - Coordinating, synthesising, integrating
    - Challenging, questioning, checking, reviewing
    - Creating, proposing, initiating
    - Supporting, nurturing, caring
    - Acting, applying

  The dominance of any one of these types will lead to an unbalanced team which will probably spend more time 'storming' than 'performing'. High performing teams are designed such that the membership is appropriate to the task – the chemistry is adjusted to ensure that the team is fit for purpose and that form follows function. Thus, it might be helpful to distinguish between structural teams which exist for organisational maintenance and task teams which are created for a specific purpose. Task teams are sometimes described as protean teams – they are created and designed to meet a specific, short-term purpose.

- *Relationships*: The team is emotionally literate – that is, it works to achieve a sophisticated level of interpersonal relationships as the primary means by which it functions. This implies that the team is conscious and deliberate in working to optimise individual and collective effectiveness. The team works in this way for both practical and moral reasons – after all, human relationships are at the heart of moral leadership, effective learning and organisational life. Effective teams are characterised by openness and candour about their working relationships – there is challenge, a willingness to discuss difficulties in working relationships and personal and professional honesty. The working style of an effective team is relaxed and supportive and every member accepts the responsibility to be engaged and to engage others. The team also cultivates the interpersonal skills that are essential to effective problem solving and decision making: listening, questioning, building and proposing, clarifying, summarising and celebrating success.

- *Trust*: The combined impact of the factors listed above creates a climate of high trust. This is reflected in the lack of formal control exercised over team members in their work with other teams in the organisation. A high degree of mutual respect ensures that relationships are based on reciprocity rather than hierarchy – that is, shared values rather than bureaucratic controls. There is a very high level of lateral communication – the team works through the creation of networks, both internal and external, and these are perceived by the team leader as a strength rather than a threat. The team is able to work through formal and informal networks and so enrich its ability to gather information and create consensus.
- *Learning*: The team is conscious and deliberate about the individual and collective learning of its members. The team's normal working procedures are used as the basis for developing knowledge, skills and experience. This is done through the review process, through opportunities to develop new skills and through the coaching and mentoring which characterises the relationships between team leaders and members. Roles are regularly rotated – there are opportunities to lead projects and exercise authority. Crucially, the team creates time and space to develop high order review and reflection and seeks to capture the knowledge it creates. It is not frightened of theory and will use hypotheses and models to review its own practices and explore new ways of working. Most importantly, the whole team works to ensure that there is shared understanding of the team's tasks and its internal processes.
- *Review*: This is one of the defining differences between a group and a team. The effective team will invest time and energy in

reviewing both what it does and how it works. It is this latter aspect that requires the greatest change from historical practice. In practical terms, it means that the team is open about its working relationships and explores strategies to improve them. The team will regularly review:

- The quality of working relationships.
- The engagement of all members of the team.
- Its effectiveness and efficiency in getting things done.
- The extent to which it models appropriate working practices.
- How far it is focused on the vision and values of the organisation.

A highly effective team will regularly ask itself the questions: how well are we doing, and how can we improve?

What is crucial about the relationship between these six elements is that they are symbiotic and mutually self-reinforcing and self-validating. Each element is critical to the success of the team and it is only in this fundamental interaction that authentic team working is possible.

Schools are staffed by one of the most sophisticated workforces in the country. The long established principles of professionalism and collegiality point to schools working as a federation of teams rather than as a bureaucratic hierarchy. The personal accountability of the head teacher remains an issue for the development of a genuine team culture. However, in the current climate, the leadership of an organisation has to be founded in interdependent relationships rather than personal autonomy. Changes have to be firmly rooted in the transformation of working relationships and structures, and teams are central to this process. The effective team can enhance performance and creativity – in fact, everything that has been written in this chapter applies as much to the learning of young people as it does to their teacher. If we are serious about organisations becoming learning organisations, then it is teams, at all levels, that are most likely to convert the principle into practice.

How authentic are the teams in your school?

How much leadership time is devoted to optimising the effectiveness of teams and developing their confidence through the real delegation of authority?

Building capacity through learning and development

The combination of effective teams and high trust has the potential to liberate leadership, not least in creating the space and capacity to move from the operational to the strategic. However, the movement from dependency to interdependency and from control to trust depends on the development of leadership potential and capacity through effective strategies for learning and development.

Figure 6.4 offers a hypothetical model of the potential impact of different learning strategies in terms of engaging with personal constructs, enabling change and increasing the potential for improving practice and so performance. The central proposition is that people are more likely to change if the strategy is personal to them and the approach is non-directive (i.e. negotiated and personalised). There is more likely to be a genuine impact on the practice of middle and senior leaders when strategies are designed to make an impact on actual behaviour – and that means changing mindscapes.

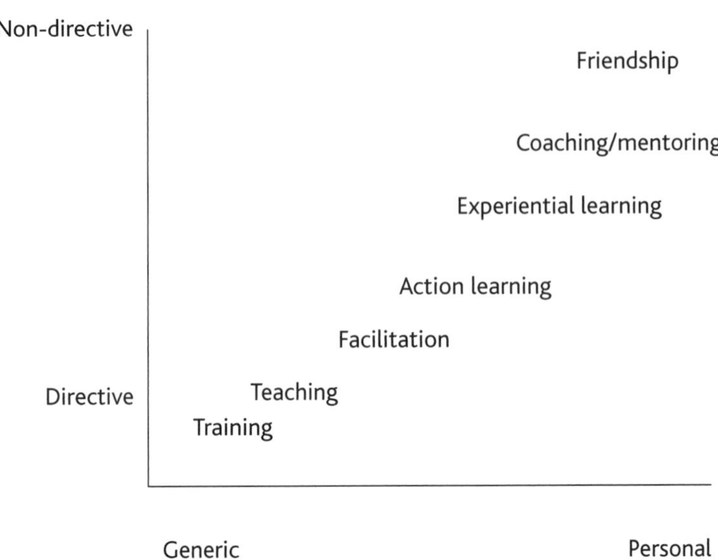

Figure 6.4. A typology of helping strategies

As we can see, generic training activities are least likely to bring about real change in the sense that they are usually directive and generic – that is, focused on the 'right answers'. While quality teaching and facilitation are significantly more likely to enable change, it is action learning and coaching/mentoring that are most likely to make an impact, in terms of reconciling theory and practice, and lead to morally appropriate action. Friendship is a seriously underdeveloped aspect of leadership learning. Most successful human beings have a significant relationship in their lives which is rooted in absolute trust, totally positive regard, deep commitment and, dare we suggest, love. This is the phone call late at night after a disastrous governors' meeting, the conversation in the pub seeking advice on how to challenge poor performance in a senior colleague or the conversation over dinner when it feels as though personal enthusiasm and drive have been lost.

> Does your personal experience confirm or challenge the model outlined in Figure 6.4?
>
> What developmental activities, in your experience, have had the greatest impact on your confidence and performance as a leader?

Action learning has a wide range of meanings and applications – action research and action enquiry are common manifestations. The following definition of action enquiry provides a very clear definition of its scope:

> Action inquiry is a way of simultaneously conducting action and inquiry as a disciplined leadership practice that increases the wider effectiveness of our actions. Such action helps individuals; teams, organizations and still larger institutions become more capable of self-transformation and thus more creative, more aware, more just and more sustainable. (Torbert 2004: 1)

Action learning is a practice-orientated, problem-solving model that works through collaborative approaches. It is based on the principle of 'learning by doing'. It combines a focus on shared problem solving, personal and group learning and is a powerful vehicle for improving performance, developing practice and supporting innovation. Because it works through genuine issues, it is perceived to be both relevant and developmental. It requires a systematic and disciplined approach and, most distinctively, the active intervention of a coach/mentor to provide support and ensure the integrity of the learning process.

Experiential learning is derived from the same conceptual framework as action learning, but it is much more focused on learning by doing the actual job. It is often most effective when the learning opportunity takes the form of a secondment, internship or consultancy. Experiential learning needs to meet a range of criteria if it is to realise its full potential:

- Experiences are carefully chosen for their learning potential (i.e. they reflect the range of possible leadership situations and encompass the potential diversity of leadership practice). Ideally they will concentrate on a specific project that is real and operates within genuine parameters of time and resources.
- Throughout the experiential learning project, the learner is expected to take responsibility for their learning – in particular, actively engaging in posing questions, investigating, problem solving, accepting responsibility and accountability and seeking feedback.
- Reflection is pivotal to the experiential learning process. This reflection leads to analysis, critical thinking and synthesis that, in turn, inform conclusions and implications for future practice.

- Learning networks are established, developed and nurtured: learner to self, learner to others and learner to the world at large.

The sorts of challenges found in experiential approaches to leadership development could include:

- Focusing on aspects of the current post that are low in terms of consistency and confidence.
- Leading a whole school project in real time with significant outcomes and appropriate resources and staffing.
- Engaging in a consultancy project for another school (e.g. the introduction of a particular learning strategy across a partnership or cluster of schools).
- Spending time in a very different type of school (e.g. all teachers in mainstream schools should spend time in a special school). Exchanges between primary and secondary and maintained and fee paying can also be instructive.
- Developing links and exchanges with schools in developing countries.
- Spending time working with schools in Eastern Europe.
- Attending international courses and conferences – often costing much the same as a one day event in London.
- Using social media to build a network of leaders in similar situations.
- Reading widely – especially outside education.
- Working with a coach to develop an analytical and questioning approach to work.

> What opportunities does your school CPD strategy offer in terms of experiential learning?
>
> Is there a strategy to provide opportunities for staff to move outside their current area of responsibility?

In the context of leadership development, mentoring/coaching is often presented as the most appropriate model because of its focus on support and learning. Team leaders need to be both coach *and* mentor, providing support for specific interventions and helping team members to develop a long-term personal and professional learning strategy.

For the purposes of this discussion, coaching, mentoring and counselling might be defined as follows:

- Coaching: A short-term intervention to provide explicit support in developing specific skills, techniques and strategies.
- Mentoring: A sustained, one-to-one relationship based on trust in which the mentor actively supports the learner to build capacity to enhance personal effectiveness.
- Counselling: A sustained, one-to-one relationship based on trust in which the mentor actively supports the learner to build capacity to enhance personal effectiveness.

One of the key insights in learning theory is Benjamin Bloom's (1984) discussion of solutions to what he calls 'the two sigma' problem. Bloom shows that students provided with individual tutors typically perform at a level about two standard deviations (two sigma) above where they would perform with standard group instruction. This means that a person who scores at the 50th percentile on a standardised test after regular group instruction would score at the 98th percentile if personalised tutoring replaced group instruction. Two sigma is therefore transformative in terms of understanding and so the potential to act. The problem is how to reorientate our current approach to teaching and learning so that the tutorial approach becomes the norm. The perceived cost of such an approach must surely be outweighed by the relative impact.

The specific characteristics of personalised tutoring/mentoring might be defined as:

- Clarifying the learner's situation and priorities.
- Supporting reflective analysis of performance and review.
- Providing feedback on actual performance based on observations and evidence.

- Implementing strategies to support problem solving or enhance performance (e.g. skill building, setting challenges, providing advice, demonstrating techniques, removing barriers).
- Providing feedback on progress, recognition and reinforcement of success and the introduction of alternative strategies (if necessary).
- Identifying factors relating to personal well-being.
- Emphasising the importance of consolidation and challenge.

> Does your experience of coaching and/or being coached confirm these broad principles?
>
> What, for you, are the key issues in developing a successful coaching relationship and a culture in school that reinforces the potential of coaching?

Three further theoretical models reinforce the potential of mentoring and coaching: the growth mindset, scaffolding and the zone of proximal development.

Central to effective feedback is developing and sustaining the growth mindset and minimising the fixed mindset. As we discussed in Chapter 4, a growth mindset is an important corollary of effective learning, irrespective of age, status or role. In fact, it could be argued that a predisposition to an essentially optimistic view of human potential, and a recognition of the importance of commitment and hard work, is fundamental to the leadership of an organisation which is committed to learning and growth. Dweck (2006: 141) maintains that to secure highly effective organisations:

> our best bet is not simply to hire the most talented managers we can find and turn them loose, but to look for managers who also embody a growth mindset: a zest for teaching and learning, an openness to giving and receiving feedback, and an ability to confront and surmount obstacles.

> If we wish children to have a growth mindset then surely their teachers need to have one too. What are the implications of this for the way in which leaders model learning relationships with teachers?
>
> To what extent is the culture in your school aspirational and optimistic?

One of the best ways to secure a growth mindset is for teachers and coaches to support personal growth and aspiration. In the scaffolding model, teachers provide graduated levels of support that help students reach higher levels of understanding and develop skills they were unlikely to achieve working alone. Just as with the scaffolding on a building, the support is gradually removed when the learner no longer needs it. Ideally, the teacher transfers responsibility for their learning process to the student step by step. As the building becomes secure, so the scaffolding can be removed. Scaffolding works by:

- Securing interest and engagement.
- Clarifying the task.
- Maintaining motivation and focus.
- Providing feedback by modelling strategies and outcomes.
- Controlling frustration and risk.
- Confirming and reinforcing success.

Scaffolding is very much about mastery teaching, in that it is a highly skilled intervention to secure the engagement and active participation of the learner and so enhance their understanding, but at the same time moving the learner from dependency to interdependent and autonomous working.

As we saw in Chapter 4, Vygotsky's concept of the zone of proximal development (Sternberg 1990: 242) describes the gap between what the learner working alone can achieve and what can be achieved with the support of a skilled helper, facilitator, mentor or teacher (see Figure 6.5). What is particularly significant about this model is the extent to which performance is enhanced by the intervention of support, so that outcomes are higher at the same level of potential or capacity. This model serves to reinforce the proposition that the key issue in leadership learning is that it has to be seen as an essentially social relationship. The potential for learning and growth is directly proportionate to the quality of the learning relationship.

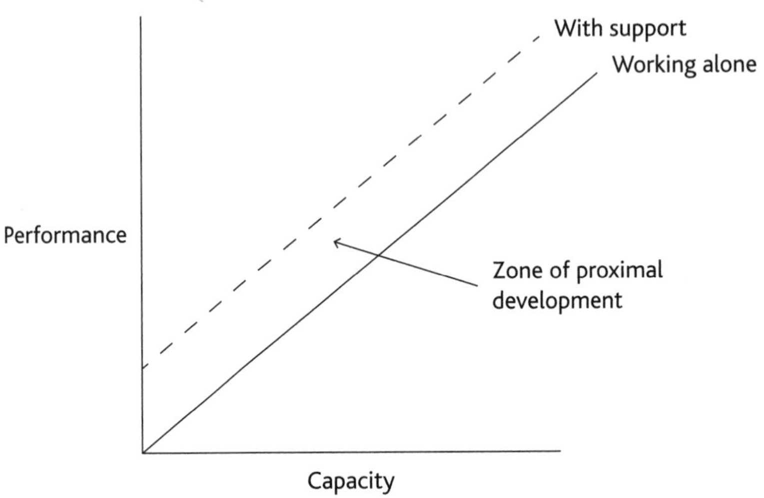

Figure 6.5. The zone of proximal development

The zone of proximal development explains why coaching and mentoring are pivotal to leadership learning and, most importantly, personal change and the realisation of potential. From the development of vital management skills (e.g. managing a meeting) to higher order leadership development (e.g. creating a high performance culture), the chances are that the one-to-one relationship is the best way to bring about deep and sustainable personal and professional change.

In summary, it seems that a number of propositions can be identified in developing a model of leadership development that integrates theory and practice and meets the criteria for ensuring appropriate (i.e. morally valid) action:

- Leadership development needs to be work based and focused on the actual job.

- Effective leadership practice needs to be analysed and understood in the context of alternative theoretical and research-based perspectives.
- Learning needs to be seen as an iterative, cumulative process in which the learner is able to develop a personal construct that is relevant to their situation and stage of development.
- Leadership development programmes should include opportunities to practise leadership on real topics in real time with appropriate resources.
- Personal engagement through coaching and mentoring in order to provide feedback and focused interventions.
- Collaboration with peers and different contexts regarded as fundamental to securing feedback and developing reflexivity (i.e. critical awareness of self and practice).
- Opportunities to take risks and to practise key behaviours and skills.
- Recognition of successful learning and reinforcement of personal change.

The combination of complex change, high stakes accountability and the moral imperatives associated with securing equity and sustained high performance all point to the need for a move away from a focus on the leader to leadership – that is, building a high trust community and developing the leadership potential of all.

Building capacity – sharing leadership

Classify each of the following components of your leadership of change as A, B, C or D, according to the extent to which it shows:

A. High confidence and is well established in principle and practice.

B. Emergent practice for some of the time.

C. Some awareness but no consistent practice.

D. No awareness.

Leadership behaviours	**Rating/ evidence**	**Implications/ action**
Recognising the underlying assumptions underpinning how you lead		
Consciously looking to move away from leader-centric ways of working		
Building trust by delegating authority and responsibility		
Working to create authentic teams		
Developing a culture of subsidiarity that includes pupils		
Seeing coaching as a key leadership strategy and an important component of the school's learning culture		
Making high impact leadership development an entitlement		
Constantly reviewing capacity across the school		
Ensuring that the leadership team consistently model all of the above		

Chapter 7

Leading through relationships

Leadership cannot function in a relational vacuum. Interaction with other people is an essential corollary of successful leadership, which can only work through sophisticated personal relationships. Effective leaders therefore have to be more than emotionally intelligent – they have to be emotionally literate and capable of working through complex relationships that move beyond the transactional. This chapter explores a range of alternative perspectives on the nature of interpersonal relationships in the context of social interaction:

- Where does your school stand on the rational–emotional continuum of leadership?
- How might we understand leadership through the relationship between love and power?
- How significant are relational trust and empathy to successful leadership?
- In what ways does your school demonstrate a commitment to care and compassion?
- How does your school develop emotional literacy across the whole community?

The case for relational leadership

Prevailing theories of leadership almost invariably place a high emphasis on the quality of human relationships as being pivotal to successful leadership. The ability to engage with people to secure commitment, consent and compliance features, in many different variants, in most definitions of the prerequisites for effective leaders. As Goleman et al. (2002: 5) express it:

> Quite simply, in any human group the leader has maximal power to sway everyone's emotions. If people's emotions are pushed toward the range of enthusiasm, performance can soar; if people are driven toward rancor and anxiety, they will be thrown off stride ... Followers also look to a leader for supportive emotional connection – for empathy.

Goleman also raises the issue that inappropriate leadership styles and behaviours can create what he memorably describes as 'toxic' organisations. There does seem to be a case for arguing that the impact of one person in the role of leader can have the sort of totally disproportionate impact that Goleman indicates. Such is the primal potential of leadership. However, it may be worth questioning why there would appear to be a paucity of leaders who understand this very basic proposition. Surely, by now, we would have learnt how to secure emotional intelligence across all forms of organisation?

> Reflect on your personal experiences of emotionally literate and emotionally dysfunctional leaders. What are the mechanisms that allow the interpersonal maturity or immaturity of one person to influence the lives of hundreds of people?
>
> Is there a causal relationship between the behaviour of school leaders and the way that teachers interpret their roles and relationships?

Given the distinctive nature of schools as (at least in theory) person centred organisations, it would seem entirely appropriate to agree with Duignan (2006: 23–24):

> A dominant theme in leadership is that it must be relational, that is, by definition effective relationships are the energy source of leadership. ...
>
> Empowering others, delegating authority and simply trusting people to get on with their tasks should underpin leader staff relationships.

Goleman and Duignan both stress the importance and centrality of the leader, and this is very much part of the western social and intellectual tradition which places a very clear stress on the significance of the individual. There is also a parallel culture of dependency and acceptance of the role and rule of the individual. This symbiotic relationship is so deeply ingrained in the literary canon of leadership that it seems totally counterintuitive to even question it. Across most organisations, there is a clear emphasis on the distinctive role and characteristics of the leader, and this is often manifested in terms of the hero-leader or the leader-centric organisation. Much writing about the relational dimension of leadership follows Goleman's model of EQ (emotional quotient) – that is, a portfolio of strategies which recognise the centrality of emotions in human interactions of any sort, with a focus on the individual who has hierarchical status and positional authority.

However, other perspectives offer a very different view on how leadership might be understood. One way of understanding the relational aspects of leadership is to think in terms of what is often described as social capital. As we saw in Chapter 5, this is about the quality of human relationships, the level of trust, the strength of social networks and the sense of being a significant part of a greater whole. Hargreaves and Fullan (2012: 90) reinforce the centrality of effective relationships in school leadership in terms of social capital, but they raise this caveat:

> Unfortunately, the development of social capital as a strategy has not yet caught on in the teaching profession ... For us social capital strategies are one of the cornerstones for transforming the profession. Groups shape behavior much more than individuals – for better or worse.

It is worth stressing that while groups are very powerful they are often dominated by individuals, and the social dynamics of schools in particular reinforce the dominance of the individual. One of the most significant components of social capital is relational trust. Bryk and his colleagues (2010: 157) demonstrate the very close relationship between the level and quality of relational trust in a school and its potential to improve:

> Absent the social energy provided by trust, improvement initiatives are unlikely to culminate in meaningful change, regardless of their intrinsic merit.

In his detailed analysis of the issues informing the emergent trends in school leadership, Earley (2013: 105) identifies a key issue, which is that while there is consensus about the importance of school leaders focusing on the 'motivation, development and well-being of staff':

> many school leaders may not have embraced the people agenda as fully as has been the case in other sectors (e.g. in the private sector where it is one of the bedrocks on which all current thinking on leadership is based).

The centrality and significance of the relational dimension of leadership is well understood and broadly accepted. However, for a number of reasons, we do not seem to be engaging with the issues involved in developing leaders with high levels of emotional literacy and a relational or person-centred orientation. This may be because there is no need – leading professionals, almost by definition, have the requisite qualities and behaviours. This idea might be reinforced by the fact that there is no consensus as to what constitutes emotional and interpersonal effectiveness, and therefore it is difficult to assess this dimension during the selection procedures that are frequently used for senior appointments in education. These concerns are further compounded by the issues surrounding the possibility of actually training or developing the relational dimensions of leadership.

Understanding relational leadership

The real issue might be that, in fact, the leader-centric approach is no longer valid or appropriate. As we have suggested elsewhere in this book, perhaps it is time to move away from the focus on the individual leader to leadership expressed as a relationship, so a school's culture and norms become more significant than personal skills and behaviours. Thus, the role of the leader is not so much to be emotionally intelligent as to espouse a culture founded on the primacy of human interaction, which is not dependent on one person's behaviour, moods and potentially dysfunctional personality. This is to shift from an immature model based on dependency to a mature model based on moving from equality to equity and the essential dignity and value of every individual. In other words, from leadership as personal status to leadership as collective capacity.

Such an approach involves achieving an appropriate balance of control and trust, task and process –or, in current thinking, love and power, strength and warmth – because these are the key determinants of all significant human relationships: partners, husbands and wives, parents and children, friends and colleagues. Getting this balance right is the essence of effective parenting as well as cooperative working in almost every social context (e.g. coaching, nursing, teaching, leading). One way of understanding how we might best engage with this complexity is to see human relationships primarily in terms of compassion. However, there is a problem with compassion as a concept because it is often seen in terms of pity and an almost paternalistic concern for another person. This is clearly inappropriate as a basis for effective personal and professional relationships:

> Might there not be another kind of compassion, one that if not joyful, is at least positive, involving not sadness and passion so much as attentive openness, solicitude, patience and listening? (Comte-Sponville 2002: 109)

This is the sense of compassion that will underpin the rest of this chapter. Our discussion will now focus on three themes which emerge from the issues raised above:

1. Is it still appropriate to emphasise the relational dimension of leadership in education in its current form?
2. Given the changing context of schools, what model of relational leadership might be most appropriate for the future?
3. What strategies are most likely to embed any alternative model of relational leadership into actual practice?

As previously discussed, for Haslam et al. (2011: 17) leadership is too often seen:

> as a noun rather than as a verb, something that leaders possess rather than as a process in which they are participants ... leader-centricity tends to obscure, if not completely overlook, the role that followers play.

This emphasis on the leader as an individual is expressed in a wide variety of ways, not least the increasing gap between leaders and followers in terms of status, remuneration and rewards. It is argued that this gap is necessary and justified because of the increasing accountability that is focused on the individual but this, of course, is actually an exacerbating factor. How can it be possible in any human enterprise, let alone a school, to identify and isolate the contribution of one individual to the exclusion of all others? There is little doubt that Duignan's view (2006: 131) is widely accepted and fundamentally true for many education professionals:

> The work of authentic educational leaders is transformational insofar as they promote and support transformational teaching and learning for their students. To do this they must bring their deepest principles, beliefs, values and convictions to their work. The ethic of authenticity is at the very heart and soul of educational leadership.

Developing an alternative model of relational leadership

Duignan's argument assumes the ability of the authentic leader to secure the engagement and commitment for transformation. It also raises issues as to the appropriateness of this view of leadership in communities that are focused on learning and, at least in theory, serve as models of democratic communities educating citizens for life in the 21st century. Not least, it raises significant questions about how to nurture and sustain such leaders. It might be that the changes in educational practice and policy point to:

- The moral imperative to secure equity for the most vulnerable.
- High stakes accountability focused on academic outcomes.
- Market-based competition.
- The increasing complexity of schools as organisations.
- Increased working through collaboration.
- The need for innovation and creativity.
- The need to work on social and economic issues.

Even in the smallest school this is a challenging agenda and one that might not be best responded to through traditional models of leadership and delegation. If the nature of schools and schooling is changing, then perhaps the way in which schools are led might need to change too. What is very clear is that the issues facing social organisations such as hospitals, schools as well as wider communities will grow increasingly complex, and as complexity grows so traditional models will become increasingly irrelevant if not actually harmful.

For Nussbaum (2013: 380), the answer is very clear – equality based on respect has to be:

> nourished by imaginative engagement with the lives of others and by an inner grasp of their full and equal humanity. The type of imaginative empathy society needs ... is nourished by love.

Nussbaum's central hypothesis is that justice is impossible without love. This immediately challenges many of the orthodoxies surrounding the moral dimension of leadership; it is love and imaginative engagement that seem to be at the heart of the creation of a just society. This takes us a very long way from 'skills for leadership' programmes and points to a very different model of leadership that is, fundamentally, much more complex and richly layered. Crucially, it moves from the focus on the individual to a focus on the community. The following discussion seeks to move away from the historical EQ model of emotional intelligence and literacy and, instead, explore alternative perspectives using different conceptual frameworks, while still recognising and respecting the neurological basis for social interaction. The key frameworks to be considered are:

- Trust
- Reconciling love and power, strength and warmth
- Thinking fast and slow
- Empathy and compassion

Trust

The previous discussion of trust (pp. 145–150) focused on what might be defined as organisational trust. Here we will consider relational trust, which seems to be a superordinate human quality and a quintessential example of the need to move from individual skills and characteristics to a culture based on shared qualities.

In essence, trust is all about building social capital, creating learning communities which are exemplified in the strength of social networks, interdependency, engagement, shared purpose, parity of esteem and genuine reciprocity. Pentland makes an important point, which warrants repeating:

> We are traders in ideas, goods, favors and information and not simply the competitors that traditional market thinking would make us. In each area of our lives, we develop a network of trusted relationships and favor those ties over others. Exchanges within this network of trusted social ties facilitate idea flow, create an inclusive vigorous culture, and are responsible for the collective intelligence of our society. (Pentland 2014: 130)

However, trust is not just about high quality relationships and the integrity of social interactions – it also has a direct impact on the performance of individuals, teams and organisations and, specifically, in schools:

> Absent the social energy provided by trust, improvement initiatives are unlikely to culminate in meaningful change, regardless of their intrinsic merit. (Bryk et al. 2010: 157)

Clearly the building of trust is a cumulative process, and this again reinforces the importance of leaders modelling trusting relationships in order to enable others to adopt alternative ways of behaving. It will be clear from all that has been written about collaborative working and systems leadership that relational trust is highly significant to this aspect of leadership. In many ways, relational trust is what we generally understand as trust in our day-to-day conversations. It is fundamental to both leadership and learning.

Bryk and Schneider (2003: 43–44) define relational trust through the following components:

- Respect: recognising the integrity of all of those involved in a child's education and their mutual interdependence.
- Competence: professional capability and the effective discharge of role and responsibility.
- Personal regard for others: mutual dependence and caring leading to a sense of interdependence and reciprocity.
- Integrity: consistency, reliability and a clear sense of moral purpose.

These elements would appear to be the antithesis of the relationships found in leader-centric situations and directly contradictory of the leader as hero. However, there is a major challenge in developing leaders who are trustworthy and who have the capacity to create high trust communities. Exhortations to trust are a direct denial of the essential nature of trust; the prospect of a leadership skills course on 'how to improve your trustworthiness' is patently nonsense.

Trust is a direct product of long-term sustained positive engagement and it only exists to the extent that it is reciprocal. Our trust in our leaders has to be directly reciprocated, otherwise it is only another function of dependency.

Power and love, strength and warmth

It would be interesting, and perhaps very salutary, to find out just how infrequently the concept of love appears in leadership development programmes, and yet it is a dominant feature of our lives in every other respect. As such, it seems very strange to explicitly exclude love and loving from discussions about key aspects of our social life, such as work and community. For Capra and Luisi (2014: 248), love is:

> an important part of our being human. To the qualities of love and altruism, we should add positive emotions like empathy, joy, happiness, gratitude, euphoria and hope.

One of the major issues facing schools is what model of organisational, social and community relationship is most appropriate to respond to the challenges of education in the 21st century. For Dorling (2015: 190), kindness should be added to the list of significant human qualities:

> Those in power in the most unequal of rich countries today, especially the UK, cannot imagine that kindness works. They see kindness as weakness. Had they been kinder, less aggressive, when they were younger and making their way in the world, they would probably not got to where they are today.

There is a real danger that the language of performativity (targets, outcomes, strategy), coupled with a draconian accountability model, will lead to language – and therefore behaviour – in our schools that is centred on power, control and efficiency more than effectiveness, attainment and achievement. If we want a society in which kindness is seen as a natural expression of shared humanity, then we need schools which, in principle and practice, are kind communities.

It might just be that a model centred on the most universal and compelling dimension of human relationships, love, is an important starting point. It might well be a very necessary antidote to the exercise of power and control found in increasingly power focused, centralised and top-down structures and processes. For Fay and Fink (1995: 128):

> One of our strongest desires is to be loved for who we are, not for how we perform. The most influential love is unconditional. If we have a sense that our magic people – those involved in our caretaking and learning – love us unconditionally, we feel established in our own right, regardless of our abilities, behaviour, or other characteristics. ...
>
> Teachers who establish a relationship of unconditional acceptance and respect with students are at a great advantage.

In his study, *Power and Love*, Kahane (2010: 12) uses a definition of the two concepts of power and love developed by the theologian Paul Tillich, who defines power as 'the drive of everything living to realize itself with increasing intensity and extensity'. Tillich defines love as 'the drive towards the unity of the separated'.

An alternative perspective and vocabulary is provided by Neffinger and Kohut (2013: 17), who talk in terms of strength and warmth:

> Strength can make people powerful, influential and important. After all strength is about getting things done. But there are things it cannot do. Strength alone can coerce but it cannot lead. Strength for its own sake is a corrosive force.

For those who focus on warmth:

> Their alternative vision is a world built on cooperation rather than competition, one of mutual understanding and dialogue that leads to consensus and peace. The virtues they hold in high esteem are compassion, patience and tolerance. (Neffinger and Kohut 2013: 17)

Layard (2005: 66) reinforces this perspective:

> We need other people, and we need to be needed. Increasingly research confirms the dominating importance of love.

The introduction of love as a key element in discourse about leadership raises many problems and challenges. Love is such a complex and subjective topic with so many levels of understanding and connotations that introducing it into the vocabulary of leadership might well be counterproductive. However:

> There is ultimately one common strand in what can make us happy: it is love. It is remarkable how we use this word. We love our spouses; we love our pets; we love doughnuts; we love playing tennis; we love Mozart; we love Venice. Towards all of these we have positive feelings that take us out of ourselves. As Ezra Pound wrote, 'What thou lovest well remains, the rest is dross.' (Layard 2005: 199)

But there might be a way forward. Classical Greek philosophy, notably Aristotle, was very clear about the alternative usages of love. Four distinct meanings were identified: agape, eros, philia and storge. Agape is generally understood as the love of god or humanity. Eros is usually seen in terms of sexual love and passion. It is philia and storge that give us a clue as to how to define love in the context of leadership.

Philia is understood in terms of friendship, the love between friends, and storge as affection between parent and child. Philia is the bond between people who share a common interest or activity and that bond is reinforced by affection. This is very much about a sense of mutual recognition and of being and belonging in community. Love, in the context of relational leadership, is expressed through a commitment to the well-being of others based on mutual respect and affection. So, the use of love in discussing relational leadership might include the following elements:

- Unconditional acceptance of the value, dignity and integrity of each individual.

- Passionate commitment to securing the happiness and well-being of all.
- Developing caring and compassionate relationships.
- Commitment to securing equity for all.
- Creating a sense of interdependence and mutual trust found through community.

The etymology of love is extraordinarily complex. There are multiple layers of meaning with much potential for ambiguity and misunderstanding, but it might be worth the risk of including it in our leadership methodology to secure the most powerful human emotion in the language of education.

> Nor can there be happiness without love ... Hence love is transparent joy, its light, its known and acknowledged truth. This is ... the secret of wisdom and happiness; love exists only as joy and there is no joy other than love. (Comte-Sponville 2002: 253)

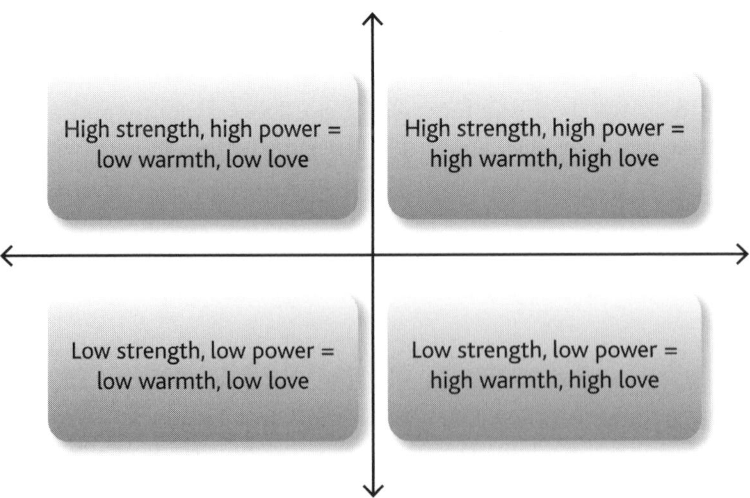

Figure 7.1. The permutations of strength and power, love and warmth

In order to understand the practical implications of the interactions of the variables in Figure 7.1, it is first necessary to clarify what they mean in context (see Table 7.1).

Permutation	Characteristics
High strength and power, low warmth and love – the hero or performance-based leader	High task completion and output orientation but disengagement and negative relationships
High strength and power, high warmth and love – the relational leader	The optimum situation – things get done by people who enjoy doing them and working together – a good place to be
Low strength and power, high warmth and love – the affiliative leader	Highly positive relationships but limited action
Low strength and power, low warmth and love – the absence of leadership	Low task and low process orientation – nothing gets done and relationships are poor – a bad place to be

Table 7.1. The permutations of strength and power, love and warmth

Of course, there may be situations where heroic leadership is called for (e.g. when the school is in crisis) and there may be times when the affiliative approach is appropriate, but it is the central argument of this discussion that it is relational leadership that should be the norm and the aspiration.

Table 7.2 shows the elements that come together with high strength and power, high warmth and love. Successful relational leadership is a complex interaction between the two sets of elements with only context to provide guidance on what the appropriate balance might be.

Positive aspects of strength and power in practice	Positive aspects of warmth and love in practice
Technical expertise and ability Justice Confidence and the willingness to act Courage and dedication Self-control Wisdom	Trust Compassion and empathy Cooperation A commitment to equity A focus on the well-being of others A belief in our shared humanity and the inherent dignity and value of all Tolerance and acceptance

Table 7.2. The positive aspects of strength and power, love and warmth in practice

On the basis of this classification of different behaviours, it becomes possible to begin to identify the implications for effective leadership. According to Kahane (2010: 129) we need to:

> become aware of our own two-sided power and two-sided love. We can think of them in different ways – as masculine and feminine, agency and communion, left and right brain ... So we must consciously and carefully observe both our power and our love and neither confuse nor choose between nor forcibly fuse them. We must learn to live with the permanent reality, outside and within ourselves, of the creative tension presented by this dilemma.

Thus, relational leadership is very much a process of developing the confidence and insight necessary to understand the tensions and dilemmas of strength and power, warmth and love. McGilchrist (2009) provides alternative perspectives on this interaction in his study of how the two hemispheres in our brains influence how we perceive and engage with the world. In his analysis, the left-brain is perceived as the logical and rational dimension (power) of our engagement with the world and the right brain as the social and emotional response to the world (love) – that is:

> a world of individual, changing, evolving, interconnected, implicit, incarnate, living beings within the context of the lived world, but in the nature of things never fully graspable, always imperfectly known – and to this world it exists in a relationship of care. (McGilchrist 2009: 174)

There is a very clear issue here in terms of developing leaders who are comfortable and confident in working in a right hemisphere world in which power and love coexist and are seen as symbiotically linked rather than as alternative perspectives. In some respects, this is counterintuitive, if not actually counter-cultural, and raises real issues about the development of leaders who are equally comfortable in both domains.

Thinking fast and slow

According to Gladwell, in his study *Blink,* we make our judgements in seconds, whether about a forged work of art, the integrity of a colleague or the emotional state of our partner. This is a justification for the caution about using interviews as part of a selection process – they are often a waste of time, simply corroborating our initial judgements. However, we seem to be very reluctant to trust this intuitive approach to thinking:

> I think that we are innately suspicious of this kind of rapid cognition. We live in a world that assumes that the quality of a decision is directly related to the time and effort that went into making it. When doctors are faced with a difficult diagnosis they order more tests. (Gladwell 2005: 13)

Gladwell's advocacy of intuition has been substantially developed by Kahneman in his work on behavioural economics. In *Thinking Fast and Slow,* Kahneman sees human thinking in two forms that he calls System 1 and System 2. More aptly, they could be called 'automatic' and 'effortful' systems, but fast and slow is a good shorthand. According to Kahneman's (2011: 18–19) description:

- *System 1* operates automatically and quickly, with little or no effort and no sense of voluntary control.
- *System 2* allocates attention to the effortful mental activities that demand it, including complex computations.

So System 1 is fast, intuitive and emotional, while System 2 is slower, more deliberative and logical. An example of System 1 thinking is detecting, without any conscious computation, that one object is further away than another, while an example of System 2 thinking is parking in a narrow space. The first judgement is almost automatic; the second requires a range of complex and integrated calculations.

System 1	System 2
Automatic	Calculated
Unconscious	Conscious
Intuitive	Reasoning
Effortless	Effortful
Fast	Slow
Emotional	Deliberate
Reactive	Rule following
Decisive	Indecisive

Table 7.3. Contrasting System 1 and System 2 thinking

Most models of leadership and management emphasise the importance of System 2 thinking, but it is Kahneman's argument that it is, in fact, System 1 thinking which is the important dimension for how we make our choices and decisions. He systematically demolishes the fallacies about how we make sense of the world and the flawed assumptions we use in our thinking about the way the world works. For example:

> Because luck plays such a large role, the quality of leadership and management practices cannot be inferred reliably from observations of success. And even if you had perfect foreknowledge that a CEO had brilliant vision and extraordinary competence, you still would be unable to predict how the company will perform with much better accuracy than the flip of a coin. (Kahneman 2011: 207)

Kahneman's work both points to the dangers of over-confidence in our decision-making processes and challenges the linked notions of prediction, objectivity and control. According to Gladwell (2005: 14):

> We really only trust conscious decision-making. But there are moments, particularly in times of stress, when haste does not make waste, when our snap judgements and first impressions can offer a much better means of making sense of the world.

It may be that we need to educate leaders to be comfortable and confident in trusting their intuition and to make judgements and decisions on the basis of what might be called wisdom or understanding, rather than the superficially rational and bureaucratic pattern of evidence and meetings that often dominates management and leadership work.

Empathy and compassion

Empathy that leads to compassion is one of the highest and most powerful expressions of love. It is the authentic response to the person in distress and an appropriate use of both love and power to alleviate, or at least mitigate, the cause of that distress. It is worth stressing that although empathy and compassion are usually associated with pain or suffering, they are also appropriate responses to having fun, feeling joyous and celebrating success. The essence of empathy is the appropriate response.

Baron-Cohen (2011: 11–12) provides a two-part definition of empathy:

> Empathy occurs when we suspend our single-minded focus of attention and instead adopt a double-minded focus of attention.
>
> Empathy is our ability to identify what someone else is thinking or feeling, and to respond to their thoughts and feelings with an appropriate emotion.

In Baron-Cohen's terms, empathy has two crucial elements, recognition and response. It is not enough to be aware of the thoughts or feelings of another person; there is also the need to respond and, crucially, to respond appropriately. This helps to distinguish between empathy and sympathy.

Daniel Goleman (2007) refers to a conversation with Paul Ekman in which Ekman identifies three types of empathy: cognitive, emotional and compassionate. The first is a purely 'cognitive' form of empathy that is 'perspective-taking'. This is being able to see things from another's point of view – putting yourself in someone else's shoes. It is important in order to better understand where someone is coming from, but it's not what we typically think of as empathy.

A second type of empathy is emotional or personal distress. This is literally feeling another's emotions. When you are watching a scary movie, and you start to empathise with the victim and feel afraid, that is personal distress in action. You are actually feeling the other's emotion through a process called 'emotional contagion'. The actor, or another person, is actually 'infecting' you with their emotion. We all experience personal distress and it is the foundation of a great deal of art, drama and music. Some people are so prone to feeling other's emotional states that they are battered about by the feelings and emotions of others (hence the label 'distress').

The third type of empathy is empathic concern. This is what we most often think about when we hear the term 'empathy'. It is the ability to recognise another's emotional state, feel in tune with that emotional state and, if it is a negative/distressful emotion, respond with appropriate concern.

Of the three, the most significant in terms of relational leadership is empathic concern, which is directly related to compassion. Compassion might be seen as the highest expression of empathy in that it involves the deepest level of identification with another person. This depth of recognition leads to similarly profound levels of commitment and the willingness to engage to alleviate the suffering of another.

Nussbaum (2013: 142–143) identifies three criteria for authentic compassion:

1. Seriousness: The person who feels compassion is satisfied that the person who is in distress or suffering is doing so in a way that is important and non-trivial.
2. Non-fault: Our potential to feel compassion is directly related to the extent to which we believe that the person's predicament is not self-inflicted or the result of conscious choice.
3. Identification: We are more likely to feel compassion to the extent to which we identify with, or feel a bond with, the suffering person. Compassion is less likely when we are unable to relate to the other person's situation.

Empathy and compassion are fundamental to what it means to be human, quite apart from any issues related to leadership. In some ways, our key moral imperatives are the result of altruistic behaviour which is driven by evolutionary advantage. There is little doubt that much of our conceptualisation of the effective leader is derived from the significance of empathy in human social life – that is, how we live in community and engage in relationships. Our assumptions about how to act in social circumstances are largely derived from the benefits of empathic behaviour – in effect, developments of the Good Samaritan model.

However, there is also a very strong case for arguing that empathy and compassion are highly practical strategies which are available to all members of a community, but especially those with leadership responsibilities. Empathic leadership is the ability of leaders to understand, relate to and be sensitive to customers, colleagues and communities. Sociopathic leadership, on the other hand, is arrogant, self-centred, insensitive and manipulative.

Empathic leadership is not, however, an easy path. For a start, it goes against the myth of the hero-leader. It's not about ego; it's about humility. It's not about fulfilling personal agendas; it's about helping clients, colleagues and communities to lead better lives. Leadership that reconciles love and power in practical compassion leads to a very different understanding of what leaders might do. Empathic and compassionate leadership has the potential to:

- Embody the moral basis of leadership in translating principle into practice.
- Recognise and respond to the essential humanity and intrinsic value of all staff.
- Enhance interpersonal effectiveness by supporting authentic understanding.
- Indicate appropriate and effective interventions and support.
- Build and reinforce trusting relationships.
- Provide a model of the behaviours necessary to create a compassionate community.

Developing intuitive leaders

The approaches to relational leadership that have been described in this chapter cannot be taught as a subject. It is not a package of skills to be delivered through a series of training events; rather, it should be seen as the development of human qualities that may not be amenable to a six-hour workshop, an online resource or an inspirational keynote.

> Virtue though it is, there's no getting around the fact that compassion is also very much a feeling; as such it is something we either do or do not feel – it cannot be called up on command ... We cannot decide to love but we can be taught to love. The same is true of compassion; it is not our duty to feel compassion, but, as Kant explains, it is our duty to nurture the capacity in us to feel it. (Comte-Sponville 2002: 116)

The answer would seem to be profound learning – that is, a model of learning that enables personal understanding by focusing on the development of intuition which, in turn, supports the development of appropriate and desired behaviours.

For example, consider what happened when you learnt to drive. Your lessons consisted mainly of three elements: developing the skills to actually control the car, learning certain key procedures (e.g. turning right, using a roundabout) and learning how to drive safely (i.e. road sense). By the time we have passed our test, most of us are 'consciously competent' – that is, we know what to do and how to do it. Within a few months, however, most of us are 'unconsciously competent' – we are driving without the need to rehearse the component parts of each manoeuvre. It is worth reflecting on just how many separate elements there are to a basic procedure such as using a roundabout. Learning to drive is essentially a process of moving from shallow to deep to profound learning. Shallow learning is knowing what, deep learning is understanding how, and profound learning is when that understanding becomes intuitive.

Profound learning is about the creation of individual meaning, the development of personal mental models and so the creation of wisdom. It is about profound personal change. Experience is processed and necessary behaviours are characterised by automaticity (i.e. we just do them). The chances are that you are reading this book on the basis of automaticity – as a result of the development of procedural memory – in exactly the same way that you learnt to drive, play the piano or listen attentively.

Two key factors seem to be essential in moving from being consciously competent to working intuitively: reflexive learning and practice. It is clear that profound learning requires hard work; in particular, sustained commitment to developing expertise. In his study of success, Gladwell (2008: 67) identifies the factors that explain the very different but equally profound success of Bill Gates and the Beatles:

> We pretend that success is exclusively a matter of individual merit. But there is nothing in any of the histories we've looked at so far to suggest things are that simple. These are stories, instead, about people who were given a special opportunity to work really hard and seized it.

The reflexive learner is someone who explores their experiences of learning to better understand how they learn and thereby improve their learning, thus becoming a more effective and successful learner both in terms of what is learnt and how it is learnt. This means that the learner is more self-aware and self-critical, more honest about themselves and, crucially, more open to positive and negative feedback. Reflexive learners need to be curious and prepared to try different approaches, motivated to improve and more able to carry through independent learning. Strategies that may help to improve and encourage reflection include self-assessment and peer assessment, learning logs, critical incident and field-work diaries, reflective commentaries and action learning approaches.

Pivotal to these processes is the importance of some form of facilitative support – the coach, mentor or tutor. One of the most significant strategies used by these facilitators who enable and support the development of profound learning is feedback, and directly related to feedback is the concept of mindset. Likewise, relational leadership is more likely to become a reality when an entire school community is engaged in the values and practices that move from the perception of leadership as personal status to leadership as collective capacity.

This chapter has sought to develop the argument for rethinking relational leadership by shifting the focus away from the emotional intelligence of individuals to creating a culture that is reinforced by the collective practice of all – the school as an emotionally literate community. We are very clear that it is necessary to develop an understanding of leadership that is focused on building trust, recognising the significance of the interaction of power and love, developing intuitive thinking and seeing the moral dimension of leadership expressed through compassion.

Leading through relationships

Classify each of the following components of your leadership of change as A, B, C or D, according to the extent to which it shows:

A. High confidence and is well established in principle and practice.

B. Emergent practice for some of the time.

C. Some awareness but no consistent practice.

D. No awareness.

Leadership behaviours	**Rating/ evidence**	**Implications/ action**
Comfortable and confident in seeing leadership as essentially relational		
Understanding the relational climate of the school		
Modelling Fullan's proposition 'Trust comes after good experiences' (2010: 97)		
Maintaining an appropriate balance of love and power		
Balancing fast and slow thinking		
Developing an empathic foundation to effective leadership		
Nurturing your intuitive responses to leadership issues		
Reviewing the quality of relationships across the school and intervening as appropriate		

Chapter 8

Leadership and personal resilience

We know that leadership is central to organisational improvement and transformation, but there is increasing evidence that the cost of leadership can be very high. Leadership can exact a significant personal, social and professional price, so it is important to understand how effective leadership is nurtured and sustained. This chapter focuses on three closely related dimensions of personal effectiveness and resilience:

1. The place of vocation in understanding leadership engagement and effectiveness.
2. The strategies that are most likely to support leadership learning.
3. The importance of personal well-being to leadership resilience.

Underpinning these themes is the core question: how do we nurture the performance, effectiveness and sustainability of school leaders?

Vocation and educational leadership

Vocation is usually seen as a key component of effective leadership to the extent that it contributes to the impact leadership makes. The variables that leadership informs might be described as explicit moral purpose, personal authenticity and sustainability/capacity.

This discussion comes down to a very simple issue: the way in which work is regarded. Is it a job to be done conscientiously but essentially in response to a salary (i.e. a fair day's work), or is it much more than that (e.g. a calling or a vocation)? It might be that a person has a job in order to allow them to follow their calling as an artist or poet. Another interpretation is that, for many people in the early days of their working life, the imperatives are financial but are gradually supplanted by the sense of developing a career and then on to a professional and/or vocational approach to work. In other words, vocation might be seen in terms of levels of engagement or commitment – that is, a move from extrinsic to intrinsic levels of significance.

Vocation	A sense of being called, personal authenticity – moral and spiritual imperatives, altruism, sacrifice, service, passion and creativity – intrinsic motivation
Profession	Integrity, dedication, discipline, specialisation, a sense of service
Career	Personal growth, enhancement
Job	Diligence, honesty, 'a fair day's work', clear boundaries, short-term engagement – extrinsic motivation

Table 8.1. Different levels of engagement with work

The danger with any model presented in this way is that the hierarchy implies varying levels of significance and virtue rather than different types of personal engagement. Instead of variable degrees of moral significance, it might be more helpful to see Table 8.1 in terms of a Maslow-type hierarchy with the emphasis on varying levels of engagement according to need, context and personal commitment. Equally, the boundaries between the various levels need to be seen as permeable and subject to change over time and according to context.

Consequently, although it is difficult to envisage, there may be circumstances where leadership is just a job. This is not necessarily to imply a negative connotation – doing a job diligently and conscientiously, but only doing the job as defined, is perfectly proper and as much as any employer has a right to expect. For many people, leadership might be best understood as career progression, usually in a large organisation where leadership is often described in terms of relative hierarchical status that is linked to varying levels of authority and responsibility. Again, there is the interesting issue that, if the job is being done effectively, then the fact that the motivation is largely extrinsic is not relevant.

> How would you characterise your engagement with your current role?
>
> Many people would argue that their response to that question would be a blend of the different levels in Table 8.1.
>
> What is the current balance of the various elements for you now?
>
> Has the ratio changed over time?

A real change in perception comes with the notion of being a professional – in many ways, the concept of professional status has much in common with the language of vocation. Indeed, one of the central criteria for professional status is a sense of duty, a moral obligation or a high level of commitment.

Of course, the worry comes with moving into a relativistic scale of moral worth – that working in this postcode area is morally more significant than that one but not as significant as that one ... Another issue with the concept of vocation is that it has very strong faith connotations. In some societies, a religious vocation seems to be superordinate by virtue of being a direct call from God. Many societies seem to value faith-based vocations more than, say, the desire to do a 'decent job' and be fairly recompensed or to work in a professional way. It is important to avoid the trap of ascribing different levels of integrity or significance to different areas of employment and seeing some as being of greater worth than others.

At the same time, it is worth stressing that those who work in response to a vocation may give more – in every sense. Their level of commitment might be higher, their willingness to accept challenging or demanding tasks or working circumstances may be higher, and their expectations in terms of recognition and reward are often substantially below social norms and expectations. Of course, vocation does not necessarily involve sacrifice, but it may. There is therefore a case for arguing that leadership is more demanding and challenging today than it has ever been. Kellerman (2015: 263) points out:

> how hard it is in this day and age to lead. One slip and you're not only down, likely you're out. The rewards of leadership can still be great, material and otherwise. But they are lesser, and the risks are greater. Leading has become a high-wire act that only the most skilled are able to perform successfully over a protracted period of time.

In this context, a higher order imperative may be very necessary to sustain engagement. In secular terms, vocation might be understood from a range of perspectives but underpinning them all will be some notion of motivation combined with social and cultural norms. Hence, vocation can be explained in terms of personal psychological drives, a focus on individual social well-being and a sense of moral purpose or social expectations. For many people, vocation will be explained in terms of the conditions of their faith and the expectations associated with serving God.

> Do you agree with Kellerman that leadership has become a 'high-wire act'?
>
> How does vocation fit in an age of what has been described as 'football club management'?

Just as a vocation is seen as 'more than just a job', so some areas of human activity are ascribed greater significance than others. Is a vocation to the priesthood a higher order calling than to be a teacher or a doctor? Are vocations to the so-called professions of greater significance than those jobs that support them (crudely, is it possible to have a vocation to be a doctor but not a nursing assistant)?

There might be a parallel in the distinction that has been drawn between being a professional and working in a professional way – professionalism. The latter is open to all as it has no connotations of relative status but rather the integrity with which we engage in work. Thus, in formal (and perhaps rather arcane) terms, a cleaner may not be a professional but may work professionally – that is, in a diligent and moral way, doing whatever tasks are required in an appropriate and effective way and, if necessary, taking extra trouble. Professionalism is often defined in terms of commitment, dedication and a sense of service to others. However, this is clearly unsatisfactory from a range of perspectives. We need to talk about vocation in terms of personal commitment rather than occupational status.

> Is vocation a useful concept in thinking about leadership in education?
>
> Are there elements of your work that do meet your criteria for a vocation?
>
> What are the characteristics of those elements compared to the rest of your job?

What seems to be true of all attempts to explain human behaviour is the central importance of personal well-being, most commonly expressed through happiness. One way of understanding vocation is in terms of 'being true to who I am' – in other words, seeing vocation as an expression of personal integrity and authenticity. There appears to be a very high correlation between personal authenticity and personal well-being, and it may be that vocation needs to be understood as an expression of a preferred future state or the optimum scenario for living a life. For Robinson and Aronica (2009: 21):

> The Element is the meeting point between natural aptitude and personal passion ... Being in their Element takes [people] beyond the ordinary experiences of enjoyment or happiness ... When people are in their Element they connect with something fundamental to their sense of identity, purpose and well-being. Being there provides a sense of self-revelation, of defining who they really are and what they are meant to be doing with their lives.

Certainly, research into personal well-being would seem to demonstrate a very high level of congruence between well-being and a range of significant variables. If well-being is defined as the optimum state for a human being – essentially, where negatives are significantly outweighed by positives – then it is possible to envisage the ideal circumstances for a human life. This view would obviously have to include work as a significant factor in determining human happiness and fulfilment. Nurmi and Salmela-Aro (2006: 186) demonstrate a range of significant correlations:

- People who report that their goals are in congruence with their inherent needs report higher well-being than those who report that their goals are incongruent with their needs.
- People who report having intrinsic goals (self-acceptance, affiliation, community feeling) report a higher level of well-being than those who report more extrinsic goals (financial success, materialism, physical attractiveness).
- People who report a high level of commitment and involvement in their goals show a high level of well-being and low distress.
- People who think they can control the ways in which their goals proceed have higher levels of well-being than those who lack belief in personal control.

This clearly raises the issue of vocation as goal orientation or the particular motivation in a person's life. In essence, vocation can be understood as the personal, subjective and motivating force that transcends all other demands and preoccupations – that is, vocation gives purpose, or in Pink's compelling phrase it is 'the oxygen of the soul' (2009: 129). As Pink points out, this sense of focus and engagement is what Csikszentmihalyi (1997: 117) refers to as an 'autotelic experience' from the Greek auto (self) and telos (purpose). It is 'something that is worth doing for its own sake ... because it contains its goal within itself' (Csikszentmihalyi 2003: 57). This may well be one of the defining characteristics of a vocation; irrespective of moral or cultural context, vocation implies an imperative, a sense of being driven or called.

What is your response to the various factors outlined above?

Robinson's idea of 'the Element'.

The factors contributing to well-being identified by Nurmi and Salmela-Aro.

'The oxygen of the soul'.

The idea of an 'autotelic experience'.

Flintham (2011: 26) makes a very explicit link between vocation as the manifestation of personal faith and working in the 'hard places to be':

> For a large majority of the sample of school leaders, irrespective of the faith perspective or context of role, the sense of call was to service in areas of social deprivation, be they disadvantaged communities of the inner city; the 'forgotten' areas of rural hardship or to those 'damaged' by personal circumstances ... a sense of call to the hard places to be ... a call to ministry as a teacher.

Either way, it is the dominant factor in a person's mindscape that becomes superordinate and determines the relative significance of other activities. This is the starving poet, the author whose first book is rejected by 12 publishers in a year, the athlete who transcends injury, the person who overcomes social and economic disadvantage to follow a personal mission. The autotelic person is:

> less dependent on the external rewards that keep others motivated to go on with a life composed of dull and meaningless routines. They are more autonomous and independent, because they cannot be as easily manipulated with threats or rewards from the outside. (Csikszentmihalyi 1997: 117)

Csikszentmihalyi famously developed this idea into his concept of flow – the total engagement of the musician, artist, athlete or any human being engaged in autotelic experiences:

> In flow, people lived so deeply in the moment, and felt so utterly in control, that their sense of time, space and even self melted away. They were autonomous, of course. But more than that, they were engaged. They were as the poet W. H. Auden wrote: 'forgetting themselves in a function.' (Pink 2009: 115)

It might be helpful to see vocation as the public outward expression of an inner private life. There is a symbiotic relationship between who I am and what I do. To deny the potential of that relationship is, potentially, to compromise a significant element of what it means to be an effective human being. On the positive side, the greater the congruity between the public and private self, the greater the potential for psychological, social and physical well-being.

Matthew Crawford works as a social philosopher and is the owner of a motorcycle repair shop. He argues very compellingly for the importance of craftsmanship and physical work over the negativity of much modern work:

> The narrow mechanical things I concern myself with are inscribed within a larger circle of meaning; they are in service of an activity that we recognize as part of a life well lived. (Crawford 2009: 197)

From this perspective, a vocation is an imperative that cannot be denied, diluted or compromised –it is essential to the integrity of the person. As Taylor (1991: 28–29) expresses it:

> There is a certain way of being human that is my way. I am called upon to live my life in this way, and not in imitation of anyone else's. But this gives a new importance to being true to myself. If I am not, I miss the point of my life. I miss what being human is for me.

For Aristotle, virtues are the basis for living a virtuous life that is, in turn, defined as living according to our nature as rational animals. We make choices and work towards the optimum balance which Aristotle defines as *eudemonia* – 'the state of being well and doing well in the state of being well, of a man's being well-favoured himself and in relation to the divine' (Taylor 1991: 148). Living out a vocation therefore might be seen as reconciling the need to be in the world with the internal need to respond to moral or spiritual imperatives.

> For a virtue is not a disposition that makes for success only in some one particular type of situation ... Someone who genuinely possesses a virtue can be expected to manifest it in very different types of situation (MacIntyre 2007: 205)

In other words, leadership in education is not confined to the school. The personal and professional qualities of the leader, underpinned by the vocation to lead, can be transferred into different situations and contexts.

> Do you feel that your work as an educational leader is allowing you to develop your full potential in a way that is personally meaningful and purposeful?

Strategies to support leadership learning through reflection

It is axiomatic to successful leadership that leaders engage in sustained professional learning. What is less clear is the extent to which certain developmental strategies actually work. Kellerman (2012: xix) captures the tension perfectly:

> ... most of those who engage in leader learning do testify, albeit subjectively, to the efficacy of their experience. Still, if Americans are so good at developing leaders, why is America in such a mess? Why are our politics so ineffectual and why is our economy so resistant to resilience? Can those of us in the leadership industry honestly say that, in the last several decades, we have had the impact we wanted and intended?

This takes us to the key issue in translating theory into practice: it is not enough just to act; action has to be morally consistent and translate aspiration into actuality. Nor is it acceptable to engage in speculative theorising – we are talking about children's lives, not angels and pinheads.

Leadership effectiveness has to be seen as the result of a learning process, one of growth and development, which engages with the interaction of beliefs and practice, and not a succession of events. For Dewey (1933: 23), the pivotal component of this learning process is reflection, which is an:

> Active, persistent and careful consideration of any belief or supposed form of knowledge in the light of the grounds that support it and further conclusions to which it leads ... it includes a conscious and voluntary effort to establish belief upon a firm basis of evidence and rationality.

If it is accepted that leadership can be learnt, then a central concern becomes the identification of those strategies that are most likely to help individuals change their personal constructs. Moon (2004) summarises the perspective that Habermas (1971) brings to the debate about the relationship between theory and practice. It is not enough to rely solely on evidence – what is required is:

> the development of knowledge via critical or evaluative modes of thought and enquiry so as to understand the self, the human condition and self in the human context. The acquisition of such knowledge is aimed at producing a transformation in the self, or in the personal, social or world situation or any combination of these. (Moon 2004: 14)

For Dewey, the emphasis was on developing modes of thought, central to which are the various manifestations of reflective practice. The crucial relationship in any model of professional work is that between theory and practice: a relationship that is essentially iterative – that is, each informs the other. It is the success of this mutual influencing that determines the integration of theory and practice. This relationship is given an interesting (and unexpected) perspective from a study on the conflict between drug traffickers and law enforcement agencies in Columbia:

> Kenny uses the Greek terms *techne* and *metis* to differentiate two different modes of learning. Techne refers to formalized knowledge – facts, figures, techniques, plans and other data that can be conveyed through lectures, field manuals and other academic training. Metis, by contrast, refers to knowledge that is gained through experience and interaction, learning through failures and successes during day-to-day operations and spread through networks of practice. (Sagarin 2012: 43)

It is interesting that the most successful law enforcement agents primarily rely on metis to maintain their effectiveness and capability and that points directly to a model of reflection and reflexivity.

A key element of reflection that bridges theory and practice is challenge. This book is designed to support conversations about challenge in teaching and learning. The central proposition is that human beings are at their most effective as learners when faced with a challenge, a problem to solve or an enquiry to follow. One way of understanding human evolution is to see it in terms of an increasing capacity to solve problems collaboratively. Challenge-based approaches are how we move from shallow learning based on the replication of information to deep learning based on the creation of knowledge, personal understanding and the ability to act and apply:

> If challenges are too high one gets frustrated, then worried and eventually anxious. If challenges are too low then relative to one's skills one gets relaxed, then bored. If both challenges and skills are perceived to be low, one gets to feel apathetic. But when high challenges are matched with high skills, then (there is) deep involvement. (Csikszentmihalyi 1997: 30)

Most human activity, whether at work, socially or at recreation, is a form of problem solving. From the solitary crossword solver or Sudoku player to team sports to reading detective novels (vicarious problem solving?), people love challenges. Some play computer games, sometimes obsessively; other people play bridge, sometimes obsessively. Most work is, in essence, sequential problem solving, usually with others. The operating theatre, the supermarket on Christmas Eve, the aftermath of a road traffic collision and getting a flight away on time all have one thing in common – people working collaboratively to solve a range of problems, some of which are habitual and others unique to that time and place.

One way to understand how we learn is the double helix. As we saw in Chapter 4, one strand is the curriculum – the content to be acquired, understood and applied. The other strand is the skills and strategies necessary to create knowledge rather than just replicate information – the cognitive curriculum. Linking the two strands are challenge, techniques and strategies – the learning process. The function of the teacher, coach or facilitator is to enable the relationship between what has to be learnt with how it is to be learnt by developing the relevant skills and providing appropriate challenges.

A crucial function of challenge in teaching is to facilitate the movement from shallow to deep learning. This is about moving from managing information to creating knowledge, from accurate replication to understanding, and the ability to apply and use that knowledge in practice. What constitutes an appropriate challenge is, of course, highly subjective. For challenges to contribute significantly to developing confidence and competence as a leader, they need to be paralleled by a range of intellectual or cognitive skills. A taxonomy of such skills for leadership might include the ability to:

- Deconstruct a challenge, identify its salient components, clarify their relative significance and prioritise them.
- Compare and contrast alternative responses and identify their potential significance and contribution.
- Explain and justify a chosen approach and defend it through the use of evidence and logical argument.
- Analyse an issue by identifying its component parts, demonstrating their relationship to each other, and explaining their relative significance and implications for practice.
- Synthesise a range of component elements and integrate them in order to provide a new explanation or to provide a meta-perspective.

- Exemplify by providing models and illustrations in order to secure understanding.
- Demonstrate the logical integrity of an argument by demonstrating the consistent application of causality, sequences, evidence and derivation through inductive or deductive reasoning (as appropriate).
- Derive valid conclusions from relevant evidence and present those conclusions in such a way as to demonstrate both their integrity and their potential to solve a problem and inform future action.
- Present all of the above in a way that uses an appropriate vocabulary, deploys evidence as necessary and uses media as is justified by the needs of the audience.
- Problematise practice – that is, to recognise that habituated professional practice is not necessarily self-legitimating and that it needs to be critically reviewed in terms of its implicit assumptions.
- Use review and reflection to develop as a reflexive practitioner.

This catalogue of intellectual skills may look rather intimidating in the context of a world where the normative is the norm and *ex cathedra* statements are accepted without question or challenge. However, they are essentially what many primary age children would recognise, in a different guise and with different levels of significance, as the key elements of the Philosophy for Children approach. Perhaps we need Philosophy for Leaders.

> Today, reflexivity must, first and foremost be understood in relation to the general societal conditions that mean that the individual constantly has to choose his or her way, not only externally, between all sorts of offers but also internally in terms of life course, lifestyle and identity. But with this, reflexivity also comes to have significance for some of the personal characteristics such as independence, self-confidence, sociability and flexibility. (Illeris 2007: 72)

Therefore, successful leaders (and people) develop the ability to reflect on their life and practice and then move on to a higher level of engagement when they become reflexive (i.e. moving from reflection into reflection-with-action).

> All human beings – not only professional practitioners – need to become competent in taking action and simultaneously reflecting on this action to learn from it. (Argyris and Schön 1974: 4)

How do you respond to the notion of challenge in leadership learning?

How open to challenge from your senior colleagues, teaching staff, governors and pupils are you?

How would you cope with a Paxman-style interview on the stewardship of your school?

Who provides the still, small voice that stands behind you whispering, 'Sic transit gloria mundi'?

Figure 8.1 shows the dynamic relationship between theory and practice and how, in a learning environment, there is a process of mutual influencing for which the primary mediating influencing process is reflection. This is very much the action learning process and is the basis for most models of coaching and models that require learners to reconfigure their mental models of themselves and their practice.

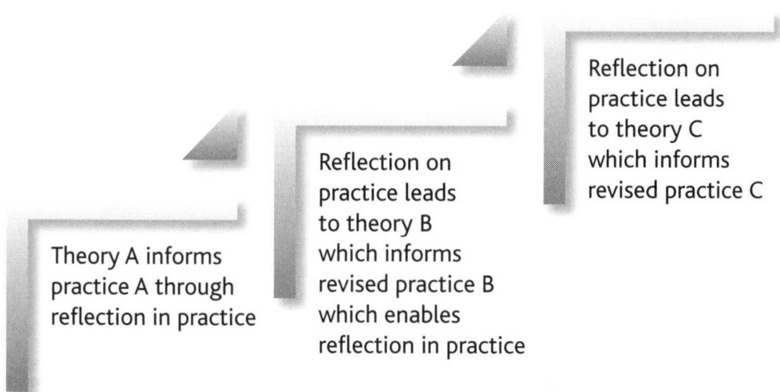

Figure 8.1. The interaction of theory and practice

A practical manifestation of review and reflection is feedback. Feedback is fundamental to any form of learning – it is how children first begin to develop language and it is how the most sophisticated professional learns to improve their practice. Feedback is essential to changing behaviour and so performance. Just as a thermostat in a central heating system works by responding to the changing environment, so feedback is a means of informing and influencing leadership behaviour. Reflective practice based on skilled feedback is a central component of leadership learning in that it enables:

- The analysis of practice to support understanding.
- Affirmation and reinforcement of good practice.
- The identification of the basis for changing behaviour.
- Confirmation and embedding of successful change.

In effect, feedback is a particular manifestation of leaders engaging in dialogue with their colleagues; it is the rich and sustained conversation about effectiveness that is one of the most powerful strategies available to a leader. Feedback following any form of observation of practice, learning project or activity provides the most effective means of translating the observation into real change in behaviours and practice. It is also a very important basis for building and sustaining high quality interpersonal relationships across the school. Effective feedback demonstrates respect and very practical support for a learner.

> Effective professional development integrates theoretical principles and practical applications ... However, theoretical content that is not linked to practical applications and rich illustration is also ineffective. (Robinson 2011: 112)

On the basis of the discussion so far, it becomes possible to offer a series of propositions about the nature of the relationship between theory and practice:

1. Theories, models and constructs are essentially personal mental models of the world (mind maps) that are often shared (the social imaginary).
2. These theories may be very simple (e.g. when and what to eat) or very complex (e.g. particle physics). The important issue is that there is no behaviour or body of knowledge that does not have a relevant personal construct.

3. Learning can be seen as the process of understanding personal theories, relating them to other theories and choosing on the basis of the most apt or appropriate.
4. A key process in reconciling theory and practice is challenge in terms of questioning established beliefs and practice and proposing alternative ways of thinking and working.
5. Converting an espoused theory into desired outcomes through action requires a commitment to action that is then mediated by review and reflection.
6. Theories are constantly modified and adapted to suit changing contexts or on the basis of feedback – 'critical and evaluative modes of thought', or what works or does not work.
7. The process of review can be understood as reflection-in-action and reflection-on-action, so translating theory into practice is an iterative process in which both change and develop.

How confident are you about the relationship between theory and practice in your analysis of your own learning and, crucially, your ability to translate theory into practice, learn from that practice and so modify the theory?

How comfortable and/or confident are you in working as a reflective practitioner?

In what ways do you model reflective practice to your colleagues through the normal daily routines of meetings, conversations and activity around the school?

Personal effectiveness and well-being

There has been an enormous growth in the quality and provision of continuing professional development for school leaders in recent years. Training and development are now more widely available than ever before, but most of that focuses on the technical and the organisational. However, there are other dimensions to sustainability that we believe are being neglected – that is, the personal aspects of well-being and wellness. This might be best understood as personal efficacy (i.e. the development of the whole person) – the recognition that leadership is more than an aggregation of technical skills and that it requires the engagement of all aspects of the person.

Personal efficacy helps us to understand a key difference between leadership and management. Although the polarisation between the two is artificial, there are dimensions to leadership that call on every aspect of the person in a way that some management tasks do not. It is perhaps best captured in the phrase of the Roman statesman, Seneca, who talked about the importance of 'cultivating humanity'. Leadership development needs to be as much about the affective as the formal.

We would argue that there are four dimensions to personal efficacy:

1. A sense of spiritual and moral purpose.
2. High quality relationships and friendships.
3. A sense of physical and psychological well-being.
4. Realising personal potential, creativity and hope.

It is important to stress that these dimensions are interdependent and that each is fundamental to the efficacy of the others. It is only when all four dimensions are developed and interacting that the full potential of leadership can be realised and sustained. If any one of them is compromised then, we believe, overall leadership efficacy is diminished and the individual is at risk. This could result in a loss of leadership effectiveness, burnout, disfunctionality and, in extreme cases, a personal or professional crisis.

> Do you accept these four elements as the basis for personal efficacy?
>
> What examples would you offer for each in terms of practical manifestations?

It is not part of the English tradition to go into these areas; the emphasis is usually on the role rather than the person, the technical skills rather than the personal qualities. However, there is an increasing recognition of Bennis and Nanus' assertion that to become a leader is to become one's self. It is not enough to develop technical competence. Equal regard has to be given to the personal because leadership is about the whole person – and to compromise this is to compromise leadership effectiveness and personal integrity. For Bennis and Nanus (1985: 21):

> the process of becoming a leader is much the same as the process of becoming an integrated human being ... leadership is a metaphor for centeredness, congruity and balance in one's life.

Peter Senge and his colleagues (2004: 186) make much the same point:

> if you want to be a leader, you have to be a real human being. You must recognize the true meaning of life before you can become a great leader. You must understand yourself first.
>
> That's why I think that cultivation, 'becoming a real human being', really is the primary leadership issue of our time, but on a scale never required before.

How much time and energy do you devote to your personal growth and development?

How often do you read a book, go to a concert or have an extended conversation with friends?

How often are you properly and appropriately self-ish?

In what ways do you 'cultivate humanity'?

This 'process of becoming' and cultivation is about developing personal resilience and sustainability, and one way of understanding this is to think in terms of a reservoir of hope:

> The 'foundations of the reservoir of hope', the spiritual, moral and ethical bases on which individual leadership stands and which provide the well spring which motivates, replenishes and renews the capacity for spiritual and moral leadership, are provided by a clearly articulated value system which explicitly or implicitly underpins leadership actions by providing the reason why. (Flintham 2011: 53)

The image created here is of a wooded valley with a dam at one end – the classic reservoir found in the mountainous areas of North Wales. When such reservoirs are full they provide a wonderful panorama of sky, mountain and water. When they are empty they have an air of desolation and sterility. Becoming personally effective and developing authenticity depends on the creation and nurturing of a reservoir of hope. Hope empowers us to take on new challenges, to make commitments, to trust and to approach the future with confidence. From hope comes courage and the desire to learn and grow.

A personal reservoir is filled by making the time and space to focus on a sense of hope, optimism, peace and personal well-being. A full reservoir enables capacity and sustainability but it needs to be nurtured and replenished. An empty reservoir leads to a loss of personal and professional effectiveness and authenticity. On some days the floodgates have to be opened and leaders have to give all day – radiating optimism and hope. At the end of the day the reservoir has to be refilled and that process is central to any notion of personal resilience. Being hopeful is about 'retaining our sense of the underlying goodness of the world', in the powerful expression of Rabbi Jonathan Sacks (1997: 267).

The effective person, and therefore the effective leader, is systematic and deliberate in filling their reservoir. Some days in schools demand non-stop giving with unremitting demands on energy and emotional resilience. Every interpersonal encounter is potentially life changing, so the effective leader devotes time and energy to ensuring that their reservoir is full:

> The personal reservoir of hope of head teachers has to be periodically refilled against the draining effect of external pressures, by a variety of replenishing and sustaining strategies, without which the implementation of the espoused value system will fail, the intensity of the motivation fade and withdrawal from the task of leading change occur. (Flintham 2011: 71)

There is no limit to the activities that might help to fill and sustain the reservoir:

- Time and space for self.
- Self-awareness, monitoring, developing personal understanding.
- Prayer, reflection and meditation, worship and liturgy.
- Time with family and friends.
- Time in community, being together.
- Lifestyle changes, balance and harmony.

- Coaching and mentoring.
- Opportunities for creativity and self-expression.
- The natural world, physical exercise, sport.
- A weekend in Venice.
- A pair of outrageous shoes.

In the final analysis, effective leaders accept responsibility for their own well-being and guard the opportunities they have to fill their reservoir. Equally, they recognise that filling their own reservoir may well be enhanced by ensuring that their team also have full reservoirs and that spending time with the team should be an opportunity to renew, refresh and replenish.

Leadership and personal resilience

Classify each of the following components of your leadership of change as A, B, C or D, according to the extent to which it shows:

A. High confidence and is well established in principle and practice.

B. Emergent practice for some of the time.

C. Some awareness but no consistent practice.

D. No awareness.

Leadership behaviours	**Rating/ evidence**	**Implications/ action**
Understanding the relationship between personal engagement and the role of the leader		
Developing and nurturing a sense of vocation		
Emphasising leadership learning and development as central to the work of leaders		
Developing the cognitive strategies to respond to the complexity and challenge of leadership		
Acting to achieve flow in work		
Ensuring that personal development is seen as part of the job, not an optional extra		
Focusing on resilience and sustainability for all members of the school community		
Developing a personal strategy to fill the reservoir		
Modelling well-being for all staff		

Conclusion

Writing this book has reinforced three key principles that underpin our thinking about leadership. Firstly, that leadership and learning are in a symbiotic relationship. Leadership in education exists to enable learning and leadership can only be effective to the extent to which the leader is learning professionally and personally. Secondly, virtually all of the ideas and principles discussed in this book apply to everyone who works in the school community, therefore the focus has to be on leadership as collective capacity rather than the status of the few. Thirdly, there has to be a balance between the technical and relational dimensions of leadership. The current emphasis on performativity and competition has to be reconciled with the centrality of effective human relationships.

There seems little doubt that in the medium to short term school leaders will have to become ever more confident in working collaboratively and securing consistently high levels of performance – both areas that require high order interpersonal skills. Equally, there is a very strong case for arguing that there is a need for 'second curve' thinking in order to address the fundamental challenges of equity, learning that is appropriate for living in an increasingly complex society and the creativity and innovation that these trends will demand of leaders.

References

Adey, P. (2012). From Fixed IQ to Multiple Intelligences. In P. Adey and J. Dillon (eds), *Bad Education: Debunking Myths in Education*. Maidenhead: Open University Press, pp. 199–214.

Adey, P. and Dillon, J. (eds) (2012). *Bad Education: Debunking Myths in Education*. Maidenhead: Open University Press.

Argyris, C. and Schön, D. (1974). *Theory in Practice: Increasing Professional Effectiveness*. San Francisco, CA: Jossey-Bass.

Asbury, K. and Plomin, R. (2014). *G is for Genes: The Impact of Genetics on Education and Achievement*. Chichester: John Wiley and Sons.

Audit Commission (2006). *More Than the Sum: Mobilising the Whole Council and Its Partners to Support School Success*. London: HMSO.

Baars, S., Bernardes, E., Elwick, A., Malortie, A., McAleavy, T., McInerney, L., Menzies, L. and Riggall, A. (2014). *Lessons from London Schools: Investigating the Success*. London: CfBT.

Barber, M., Whelan, F. and Clark, M. (2010). *Capturing the Leadership Premium: How the World's Top School Systems are Building Leadership Capacity for the Future*. London: McKinsey & Co.

Baron-Cohen, S. (2011). *Zero Degrees of Empathy: A New Theory of Human Cruelty and Kindness*. London: Allen Lane.

Battle, M. (1997). *Reconciliation: The Ubuntu Theology of Desmond Tutu*. Cleveland, OH: Pilgrim Press.

Belbin, M. (1981). *Management Teams: Why They Succeed or Fail*. Oxford: Heinemann.

Bennis, W. and Nanus, B. (1985). *Leaders: The Strategies for Taking Charge*. New York: Harper and Row.

Blakemore, S.-J. (2012). The Mysterious Workings of the Adolescent Brain [video], *TED.com* (June). Available at: https://www.ted.com/talks/sarah_jayne_blakemore_the_mysterious_workings_of_the_adolescent_brain.

Blakemore, S.-J. and Frith, U. (2005). *The Learning Brain: Lessons for Education*. Oxford: Blackwell.

Bloom, B. (1984). The 2 Sigma Problem: The Search for Methods of Group Instruction as Effective as One-to-One Tutoring, *Educational Researcher* 13(6): 4–16.

Bottery, M. (2004). *The Challenges of Educational Leadership*. London: PCP.

Brown, A. (2014). *The Myth of the Strong Leader: Political Leadership in the Modern Age*. London: Bodley Head.

Bryk, A. S., Bender Sebring, P., Allensworth, E., Luppescu, S. and Easton, J. Q. (2010). *Organizing Schools for Improvement: Lessons from Chicago*. Chicago, IL: University of Chicago Press.

Bryk, A. S. and Schneider, B. (2003). Trust in Schools: A Core Resource for School Reform, *Educational Leadership* 60(6): 40–45.

Capra, F. and Luisi, P. L. (2014). *The Systems View of Life: A Unifying Vision*. Cambridge: Cambridge University Press.

Carr, W. and Kemmis, S. (2006). *Becoming Critical: Knowing Through Action Research*. Abingdon: Routledge.

Clifton, J. and Cook, W. (2012). *A Long Division: Closing the Attainment Gap in England's Secondary Schools*. London: IPPR.

Comte-Sponville, A. (2002). *A Short Treatise on the Great Virtues: The Uses of Philosophy in Everyday Life*. London: William Heinemann.

Covey, S. R. (1992). *Principle-Centered Leadership*. New York: Simon & Schuster.

Covey, S. R. (2006). *The Speed of Trust: The One Thing That Changes Everything*. London: Simon & Schuster.

Crawford, M. (2009). *The Case for Working With Your Hands, Or Why Office Work Is Bad for Us and Fixing Things Feels Good*. London: Viking.

Csikszentmihalyi, M. (1997). *Finding Flow: The Psychology of Engagement with Everyday Life*. New York: Basic Books.

Csikszentmihalyi, M. (2003). *Good Business: Leadership, Flow, and the Making of Meaning*. London: Viking Books.

Cummings, T. and Keen, J. (2008). *Leadership Landscapes*. Basingstoke: Palgrave Macmillan.

Day, C., Sammons, P., Hopkins, D., Harris, A., Leithwood, K. and Gu, Q. (2009). *The Impact of School Leadership on Pupil Outcomes*. Nottingham: DCSF.

de Geus, A. (1997). *The Living Company*. London: Nicholas Brealey Publishing.

de Waal, F. (2009). *The Age of Empathy: Nature's Lessons for a Kinder Society*. London: Souvenir Press.

Desforges, C. (2004). Collaboration: Why Bother? *Nexus* 3: 6–7.

Desforges, C. with Abouchaar, A. (2003). *The Impact of Parental Involvement, Parental Support and Family Education on Pupil Achievements and Adjustment: A Literature Review*. Research Report RR433. Nottingham: DfES.

Dewey, J. (1933). *How We Think*. New York: Houghton Mifflin.

Diamond, J. (2005). *Collapse: How Societies Choose to Fail or Succeed*. New York: Penguin.

Dorling, D. (2015). *Inequality and the 1%*. London: Verso.

Duignan, P. (2006). *Educational Leadership: Key Challenges and Ethical Tensions*. Cambridge: Cambridge University Press.

Dunbar, R. (2010). *How Many Friends Does One Person Need? Dunbar's Number and Other Evolutionary Quirks*. London: Faber & Faber.

Dweck, C. (2006). *Mindset: The New Psychology of Success*. New York: Ballantine Books.

Earley, P. (2013). *Exploring the School Leadership Landscape: Changing Demands, Changing Realities*. London: Bloomsbury.

Edgar, D. (2001). *The Patchwork Nation: Rethinking Government, Rebuilding Community*. Sydney: HarperCollins.

Education Select Committee (2013). *Fourth Report: School Partnerships and Cooperation, Vol. I*. HC 2013–2014. Available at: http://www.publications.parliament.uk/pa/cm201314/cmselect/cmeduc/269/26902.htm.

Fay, J. and Fink, D. (1995). *Teaching with Love and Logic*. Golden, CO: Love and Logic Press.

Flintham, A. (2011). *Reservoirs of Hope: Sustaining Spirituality in School Leaders*. Newcastle-upon-Tyne: Cambridge Scholars Publishing.

Fullan, M. (2010). *All Systems Go: The Change Imperative for Whole System Reform*. Thousand Oaks, CA: Corwin.

Gardner, H. (1999). *The Disciplined Mind: What All Students Should Understand*. New York: Simon & Schuster.

Gardner, H. (2006). *Five Minds for the Future*. Boston, MA: Harvard Business School Press.

Garner, R. (2015). Finland Schools: Subjects Scrapped and Replaced with 'Topics' as Country Reforms Its Education System, *The Independent* (20 March). Available at: http://www.independent.co.uk/news/world/europe/finland-schools-subjects-are-out-and-topics-are-in-as-country-reforms-its-education-system-10123911.html.

Gawande, A. (2009). *The Checklist Manifesto: How to Get Things Right*. London: Profile Books.

Giroux, H. A. (1997). *Pedagogy and the Politics of Hope: Theory, Culture, and Schooling*. New York: Westview Press.

Gladwell, M. (2005). *Blink: The Power of Thinking Without Thinking*. London: Allen Lane.

Gladwell, M. (2008). *Outliers: The Story of Success*. London: Allen Lane.

Goldacre, B. (2013). *Building Evidence Into Education*. London: DfE.

Goleman, D. (1996). *Emotional Intelligence: Why It Can Matter More Than IQ*. London: Bloomsbury.

Goleman, D. (2007). Three Kinds of Empathy: Cognitive, Emotional, Compassionate (12 June). Available at: http://www.danielgoleman.info/three-kinds-of-empathy-cognitive-emotional-compassionate/.

Goleman, D., Boyatzis, R. and McKee, A. (2002). *The New Leaders: Transforming the Art of Leadership*. London: Little Brown.

Gompertz, W. (2015). *Think Like an Artist … and Lead a More Creative, Productive Life*. London: Penguin.

Greene, J. (2013). *Moral Tribes: Emotion, Reason, and the Gap Between Us and Them*. New York: Penguin.

Habermas, J. (1971). *Knowledge and Human Interests*. London: Heinemann.

Hallam, S. and Parsons, S. (2014). Does Streaming Have an Impact on Attainment at Key Stage 1 in the Primary School? Paper presented at the British Educational Research Association conference, Institute of Education, University of London, 25 September.

Handy, C. (2015). *The Second Curve: Thoughts on Reinventing Society*. London: Random House.

Hargreaves, A., Boyle, A. and Harris, A. (2014). *Uplifting Leadership: How Organizations, Teams, and Communities Raise Performance*. San Francisco, CA: Jossey-Bass.

Hargreaves, A. and Fink, D. (2006). *Sustainable Leadership*. San Francisco, CA: Jossey-Bass.

Hargreaves, A. and Fullan, M. (2012). *Professional Capital: Transforming Teaching in Every School*. Abingdon: Routledge.

Hargreaves, A., Halász, G. and Pont, B. (2008). The Finnish Approach to System Leadership. In B. Pont, D. Nusche and D. Hopkins (eds), *Improving School Leadership*, Vol. 2: *Case Studies on System Leadership*. Paris: OECD, pp. 69–101.

Hargreaves, A., Harris, A., Boyle, A., Ghent, K., Goodall, J., Gurn, A., McEwen, L., Reich, M. and Stone-Johnson, C. (2010). *Performance Beyond Expectations*. Nottingham: NCSL.

Hargreaves, D. (2011). *Leading a Self-Improving School System*. Nottingham: NCSL.

Harris, A. (2014). *Distributed Leadership Matters: Perspectives, Practicalities, and Potential*. Thousand Oaks, CA: Corwin.

Haslam, A., Reicher, S. and Platow, M. (2011). *The New Psychology of Leadership: Identity, Influence and Power*. Hove: Psychology Press.

Hattie, J. (2009). *Visible Learning: A Synthesis of Over 800 Meta-Analyses Relating to Achievement*. Abingdon: Routledge.

Higgins, S., Kokotsaki, D. and Coe, R. (2011). *Toolkit of Strategies to Improve Learning: Summary for Schools Spending the Pupil Premium*. London: Sutton Trust–Education Endowment Foundation.

Holloway, R. (2004). *Godless Morality: Keeping Religion Out of Ethics*. Edinburgh: Canongate.

Hutchings, M., Francis, B. and Kirby, B. (2015). *Chain Effects 2015: The Impact of Academy Chains on Low Income Students*. London: Sutton Trust.

Illeris, K. (2007). *How We Learn: Learning and Non-Learning in School and Beyond*. Abingdon: Routledge.

Judt, T. (ed.) (2002). Introduction. In A. Camus, *The Plague*. London: Penguin Modern Classics.

Jukes, I., McCain, T. and Crockett, L. (2010). *Understanding the Digital Generation: Teaching and Learning in the New Digital Landscape*. Kelowna, BC: 21st Century Fluency Project.

Kahane, A. (2010). *Power and Love: A Theory and Practice of Social Change*. San Francisco, CA: Berrett-Koehler.

Kahneman, D. (2011). *Thinking, Fast and Slow*. London: Allen Lane.

Kellerman, B. (2012). *The End of Leadership*. New York: HarperCollins.

Kellerman, B. (2015). *Hard Times: Leadership in America*. Stanford, CA: Stanford Business Books.

Laloux, F. (2014). *Reinventing Organizations: A Guide to Creating Organizations Inspired by the Next Stage in Human Consciousness*. Brussels: Nelson Parker.

Law, S. (2006). *The War for Children's Minds*. Abingdon: Routledge.

Layard, R. (2005). *Happiness: Lessons from a New Science*. London: Allen Lane.

Leithwood, K., Harris, A. and Strauss, T. (2010). *Leading School Turnaround: How Successful Leaders Transform Low-Performing Schools*. San Francisco, CA: Jossey-Bass.

Lieberman, M. (2013). *Social: Why Our Brains Are Wired to Connect*. Oxford: Oxford University Press.

Linsky, M. and Lawrence, J. (2011). Adaptive Challenges for School Leadership. In H. O'Sullivan and J. West-Burnham (eds), *Leading and Managing Schools*. London: Sage, pp. 3–15.

MacAskill, W. (2015). *Doing Good Better: Effective Altruism and a Radical New Way to Make a Difference*. London: Guardian Books.

MacBeath, J. (2004). *The Leadership File*. Glasgow: Learning Files Scotland.

McGilchrist, I. (2009). *The Master and His Emissary: The Divided Brain and the Making of the Western World*. London: Yale University Press.

MacIntyre, A. (2007). *After Virtue: A Study in Moral Theory*. London: Bloomsbury.

McKnight, A. (2015). *Downward Mobility, Opportunity Hoarding and the 'Glass Floor'*. London: Social Mobility and Child Poverty Commission.

Marmot, M. (2015). *The Health Gap: The Challenge of an Unequal World*. London: Bloomsbury.

Marsh, H. (2015). *Do No Harm: Stories of Life, Death, and Brain Surgery*. London: Weidenfeld and Nicolson.

Matthews, B. (2012). Playing with Emotions: Why Emotional Literacy Trumps Emotional Intelligence. In P. Adey and J. Dillon (eds), *Bad Education: Debunking Myths in Education*. Maidenhead: Open University Press, pp. 245–262.

Miller, P. (2010). *Smart Swarm*. London: Collins.

Milligan, B. (2015). Gender Pay Gap Almost Unchanged, Says ONS, *BBC* (18 November). Available at: http://www.bbc.co.uk/news/business-34855056.

Moon, J. A. (2004). *Reflection in Learning and Professional Development: Theory and Practice*. Abingdon: RoutledgeFalmer.

Moreno, M., Mulford, B. and Hargreaves, A. (2007). *Trusting Leadership: From Standards to Social Capital*. Nottingham: NCSL.

Neffinger, J. and Kohut, M. (2013). *Compelling People: The Hidden Qualities That Make Us Influential*. London: Piatkus.

Noguera, P. (2008). *The Trouble with Black Boys ... And Other Reflections on Race, Equity, and the Future of Public Education*. San Francisco, CA: Jossey-Bass.

Nurmi, J. E. and Salmela-Aro, K. (2006). What Works Makes You Happy: The Role of Personal Goals in Life-Span Development. In M. Csikszentmihalyi and I. S. Csikszentmihalyi (eds), *A Life Worth Living: Contributions to Positive Psychology*. Oxford: Oxford University Press, pp. 182–199.

Nussbaum, M. (2013). *Political Emotions: Why Love Matters for Justice*. Cambridge, MA: Bellnap Press.

O'Connor, R. (2015). Finland to Remove Cursive Handwriting from Education Curriculum, *The Independent* (3 February). Available at: http://www.independent.co.uk/news/education/education-news/finland-to-remove-cursive-handwriting-from-education-curriculum-10021942.html.

Ofsted (2015). *School Inspection Handbook* (September). Ref: 150066. Available at: https://www.gov.uk/government/publications/school-inspection-handbook-from-september-2015.

Organisation for Economic Co-operation and Development (OECD) (2015). *Education Policy Outlook 2015*. Paris: OECD.

Pentland, A. (2014). *Social Physics: How Good Ideas Spread – The Lessons from a New Science*. London: Scribe Publications.

Perkins, D. (1995). *Outsmarting IQ: The Emerging Science of Learnable Intelligence*. New York: Free Press.

Pink, D. (2008). *A Whole New Mind: Why Right-Brainers Will Rule the Future*. Singapore: Marshall Cavendish.

Pink, D. (2009). *Drive: The Surprising Truth About What Motivates Us*. Edinburgh: Canongate.

Pinker, S. (2015). *The Village Effect: How Face-to-Face Contact Can Make Us Healthier, Happier, and Smarter*. London: Atlantic Books.

Pont, B., Nusche D. and Hopkins, D. (2008). *Improving School Leadership*, Vol. 2: *Case Studies on System Leadership*. Paris: OECD.

PricewaterhouseCoopers LLP (2007). Independent Study into School Leadership. Ref: RB818. Nottingham: DfES.

Putnam, R. D. (2000). *Bowling Alone: The Collapse and Revival of American Community*. New York: Simon & Schuster.

Putnam, R. D. (2015). *Our Kids: The American Dream in Crisis*. New York: Simon & Schuster.

Ridley, M. (2015). *The Evolution of Everything: How New Ideas Emerge*. London: Fourth Estate.

Robinson, K. (2013). *Finding Your Element: How to Discover Your Talents and Passions and Transform Your Life*. London: Allen Lane.

Robinson, K. with Aronica, L. (2009). *The Element: How Finding Your Passion Changes Everything*. London: Allen Lane.

Robinson, V. M. J. (2011). *Student-Centered Leadership*. San Francisco, CA: Jossey-Bass.

Rock, D. (2008). SCARF: A Brain-Based Model for Collaborating With and Influencing Others, *Neuroleadership Journal* 1(1): 44–52.

Sabates, R. and Dex, S. (2012). Multiple Risk Factors in Young Children's Development. CLS Cohort Studies Working Paper 2012/1. London: Institute of Education.

Sacks, J. (1997). *The Politics of Hope*. London: Jonathan Cape.

Sagarin, R. (2012). *Learning from the Octopus: How Secrets from Nature Can Help Us Fight Terrorist Attacks, Natural Disasters, and Disease*. New York: Basic Books.

Sahlberg, P. (2015). *Finnish Lessons 2.0: What Can the World Learn from Educational Change in Finland?* (2nd edn). New York: Teachers' College Press.

Saxenian, A. (1996). *Regional Advantage: Culture and Competition in Silicon Valley and Route 128*. Cambridge, MA: Harvard University Press.

Schneider, M. and Stern, E. (2010). The Cognitive Perspective on Learning: Ten Cornerstone Findings. In H. Dumont, D. Istance and F. Benavides (eds), *The Nature of Learning: Using Research to Inspire Practice*. Paris OECD, pp. 69–90.

Sebba, J. and Robinson, C. (2010). *Evaluation of UNICEF UK's Rights Respecting School Award: Final Report*. London: UNICEF.

Senge, P., Scharmer, C. O., Jaworski, J. and Flowers, B. S. (2004). *Presence: Human Purpose and the Field of the Future*. New York: Currency Books.

Sergiovanni, T. (1992). *Moral Leadership: Getting to the Heart of School Improvement*. San Francisco, CA: Jossey-Bass.

Sergiovanni, T. (2005). *Strengthening the Heartbeat: Leading and Learning together in Schools*. San Francisco, CA: Jossey-Bass.

Singer, P. (1972). Famine, Affluence, and Morality, *Philosophy and Public Affairs* 1(3): 229–243.

Singer, P. (2015). *The Most Good You Can Do: How Effective Altruism Is Changing Ideas About Living Ethically*. New Haven, CT: Yale University Press.

Sternberg, R. J. (1990). *Metaphors of Mind: Conceptions of the Nature of Intelligence*. Cambridge: Cambridge University Press.

Strand, S. (2014). Even at Best Schools, Kids on Free School Meals are Performing Worse Than Their Peers, *The Conversation* (23 September). Available at: https://theconversation.com/even-at-best-schools-kids-on-free-school-meals-are-performing-worse-than-their-peers-32006.

Susskind, R. and Susskind, D. (2015). *The Future of the Professions: How Technology Will Transform the Work of Human Experts*. New York: Oxford University Press.

Syed, M. (2015). *Black Box Thinking: The Surprising Truth About Success*. London: John Murray.

Tapscott, D. and Williams, A. (2006). *Wikinomics: How Mass Collaboration Changes Everything*. London: Atlantic Books.

Taylor, C. (1991). *The Ethics of Authenticity*. Cambridge, MA: Harvard University Press.

Taylor, C. (2004). *Modern Social Imaginaries*. Durham, NC: Duke University Press.

Torbert, B. (2004). *Action Inquiry: The Secret of Timely and Transforming Leadership*. San Francisco, CA: Berrett-Koehler.

Waters, M. (2013). *Thinking Allowed: On Schooling*. Carmarthen: Independent Thinking Press.

Wenger, E. (1998) *Communities of Practice: Learning, Meaning, and Identity*. Cambridge: Cambridge University Press.

Wrigley, T., Thomson, P. and Lingard, B. (eds) (2012). *Changing Schools: Alternative Ways to Make a Difference*. Abingdon: Routledge.

Wrigley, T., Thomson, P. and Lingard, B. (2012). Resources for Changing Schools: Ideas In and For Practice. In T. Wrigley, P. Thomson and B. Lingard (eds), *Changing Schools: Alternative Ways to Make a Difference*. Abingdon: Routledge, pp. 194–214.

About the authors

Libby Nicholas is Chief Executive of the Reach4 Academy Trust. She was previously Regional Director – South and West – for the Academies Enterprise Trust. She has wide experience of headship and senior leadership in the independent and maintained sectors and across the full age range of schools.

John West-Burnham is an independent writer, teacher and consultant in education leadership. John is the author, co-author or editor of many books including *Rethinking Educational Leadership* and *Leadership Dialogues* and he has worked in 27 countries. He is a director of three academy trusts and a trustee of two educational charities. John is Honorary Professor of Educational Leadership at the University of Worcester.

Index